FEELING GOOD FOR LIFE

Feeling Good for Life

▼

The Clinically Proven Exercise and Diet System

That Will Help You Burn Fat, Build Muscle,

Boost Your Mood, and Conquer Depression

Marcos R. Salazar, B.A., CPT, JGSI

Writers Club Press
San Jose New York Lincoln Shanghai

Feeling Good for Life
The Clinically Proven Exercise and Diet System That Will Help
You Burn Fat, Build Muscle, Boost Your Mood, and Conquer Depression

Writers Club Press
an imprint of iUniverse, Inc.

For information address:
iUniverse, Inc.
5220 S. 16th St., Suite 200
Lincoln, NE 68512
www.iuniverse.com

This book is written as a source of information only. The information contained in this book should by no means be considered a substitute for the advice of a qualified medial professional, who should be consulted when beginning a new exercise, diet, or any other health program. If you are taking medication, you should consult with your physical before beginning any of the programs outlined in this book. All efforts have been made of ensure the accuracy of the information provided in this book as of the date of publication. The author or publisher expressly disclaims responsibility for any adverse effects arising from the use or application of the information contained hear in.

Cover design by Pneuma Books **www.pneumabooks.com**

ISBN: 0-595-20782-0

Printed in the United States of America

To Mom and Dad…you two gave me

the greatest gifts parents can give to a child:

Freedom and Trust. Freedom to pursue

all my dreams and Trust in the decisions

I made to achieve those dreams. I thank you

from the bottom of my heart.

Contents

Acknowledgements

To mom and dad for supporting all my crazy dreams and ideas. I don't know what I did to deserve parents like you. I would like to think Richard for believing in a 21 year old who wanted to pursue something that some said was not possible. You have been a wonderful mentor and a good friend. I feel very fortunate to have met you on this journey of mine. To Neil Ross, another who believed in the power of this life changing knowledge. Your continued assistance after our working relationship ended is greatly appreciated.

Thank you George for introducing me to weight training. Although you may not know it, you working out, your old bodybuilding magazines, and your rusted weights that became my first gym lit the spark of my love for exercise. Thanks Rosina for spending all those hours posing until we got the pictures right. You are a smart and wonderful woman and I look forward to seeing all the amazing things you will accomplish.

A thanks goes out to the staff at Bally Total Fitness and Cambridge Racquet and Fitness Club. I learned a great deal working with you guys. My experiences at the gym gave me the skills needed to enhance the exercise sections of this book. Thank you Northside Health and Fitness for allowing me to use the facility for the pictures in this book. Thanks DR3 for the pictures.

Thank you Beth Olivares from the McNair Program at the University of Rochester. This program is where I first fell in love with research and formed the vision of taking all this valuable information out of academia and putting it into the hands of the people who need it. To Mr. Gilroy for exposing me to the wonderful world of biology. Many of the ideas I have presented in this book were formulated way back in 11th grade listening to your great lectures. How I miss your jolly laugh echoing through the halls of the high school. To Mrs. Jenkins, I thank you for being the teacher who first introduced me to the art of writing.

To the Taos High School Librarians for letting me use the computers when mine broke down. Thank you Pneuma Design (pneumadesign.com) for the wonderful cover. It represents exactly what *Feeling Good for Life* is. Thank you Cha Cha for letting me use your printer and thanks Monica and John for the computer and printer. And a last thanks to all my family for the love and support you have given me all these years.

Contributors

Richard P. Halgin is a Professor of Psychology at the University of Massachusetts at Amherst. He is a licensed and board certified clinical psychologist, who has published three leading works in abnormal psychology and dozens of articles in the field of traditional and alternative mental health strategies. Some of his published work has focused specifically on the effects of physical exercise on emotional well being and cognitive functioning. He maintains an active psychotherapy practice in Amherst, Massachusetts.

Introduction

A few years ago while conducting research at the University of Rochester, I came across a research article by Dr. John Greist entitled, *Running as a Treatment for Depression*. As an exercise enthusiast, this article caught my attention; I always knew that exercise relived stress and anxiety, but I was unaware that it could be used as a treatment for depression. To my surprise, the results of this study showed that exercise was just as effective as psychotherapy in improving mood and helping people with depression overcome their feelings of sadness and gloom. This prompted me to see if there was any more research on the topic and, sure enough I found an overwhelming amount of studies conducted over the past 20 years demonstrating that exercise produces powerful mood-elevating effects and has the ability to prevent and alleviate symptoms of clinical depression. When I found out about all this research, I couldn't help but think how strange it was that I had never heard about it before.

Over the following weeks, I proceeded to ask my friends and colleagues if they knew about this strong connection between exercise and mental health. A handful of them said they knew exercise could make people feel better, but most of them had no idea that exercise was so powerful that it could be used as a treatment for depression. I continued to ask more people if they knew about this research and with each surprised look I received, the agony I felt inside grew increasingly painful. I kept asking myself, "Why don't more people know about this life-changing knowledge?" All I could think was how this valuable information could help so many people afflicted with this emotional virus. At that moment, I realized that I needed to create some type of solution that would not only inform people about the fact that exercise can elevate mood and conquer depression, but also explain how anyone can apply this amazing research to their own life. However, before I figured out how I was going to accomplish this, I had to get down to the bottom of one mystery: Why was it that so few people knew about this powerful information even though it had been available for over 20 years? I soon found the answer to this question in researching another interest of mine.

While looking at the current books and research articles on diet and nutrition, I uncovered a strange phenomenon in the evolution of the way this information eventually reached the general public: Much of the research being written about today has been available to people since the 1980s. When I discovered this, the first question that came to my mind was, "Why didn't people start utilizing this research when it was initially published?" In doing some more investigating, I soon figured out the answer—in the 1980s there were no authoritative books that discussed the research on diet and nutrition. It wasn't until many years later that someone finally decided to gather all this information and include it in a book for the general public.

Well, the research on the powerful mood-elevating effects of exercise is in the same situation as the research on diet and nutrition was in during the 1980s: there is a vast amount of research demonstrating the mood-boosting, antidepressant effect of exercise, yet there is not a single book that covers this research and incorporates it into an easy-to-use-system for people to apply to their own lives. And this is exactly why I created *Feeling Good for Life*.

Feeling Good for Life represents the dawn of a new era in the way the "blues" will be treated from now on. Researchers around the world have consistently demonstrated that exercise, psychotherapy, and antidepressant medication are equally effective when it comes to improving your mood and fighting symptoms of depression. Even more amazing is that exercise has been shown to be more effective then popular antidepressant drugs such as Zoloft in preventing depression from retuning! What I have done is gathered together all these years of research and integrated it into an innovative exercise system I call the *Feeling Good for Life* Exercise Solution. How does this groundbreaking new intervention produce such powerful mood-elevating effects?

The *Feeling Good for Life* Exercise Solution achieves this by harnessing the power of your body's natural antidepressant medicines as well as strengthens your mind psychologically. First, exercise has potent serotonin boosting effects, providing relief similar to popular antidepressant medications like Prozac and Zoloft. Exercise also enhances other vital chemicals and hormones such as endorphins and insulin, low levels of which have been shown to be involved in the development of depression. Next, exercise elevates your mood by strengthening your mind and the way you think. Because you are taking initiative and assuming responsibility for your mental health, your feelings of self-worth will improve. Things that used to cause you stress will seem more manageable to deal with. You will notice that once you begin *Feeling Good for Life,* you will have increased energy, alertness, and concentration. You will also unlock you body's potential to burn fat and build muscle, which will give you that trimmer looking physique you've always wanted. Your new body will improve your self-image and help you gain back your self-esteem and self-confidence. But more importantly, each time you go out and exercise, you will be disciplining yourself to take control of your mind and emotions by taking control of your body. The new mental power you gain through exercise will soon proliferate and flow into other areas of your life, causing you to have a much more positive outlook on the world. This extraordinary one-two physiological/psychological combination is what makes the *Feeling*

Good for Life Exercise Solution such a powerful antidepressant and puts it at an advantage over traditional treatments.

Harnessing the power of exercise alone will help you dispel the black cloud from your sky however, there is also a second component to *Feeling Good for Life* that can accelerate the wonderful benefits you will experience on your *Feeling Good for Life* Exercise Solution. Researchers are now realizing that what you eat can have a significant impact on your mental health. More importantly, the absence of certain nutrients can actually cause you to develop depression. Because nutrition plays such a crucial role in influencing the way we feel, I have developed the mood-elevating antidepressant diet *Nutrition-4-Life*. At the heart of *Nutrition-4-Life* is the *40-40-20 Solution,* which is a specially formulated combination of protein, carbohydrates, and fat that will help stabilize insulin levels and put you in the ultimate mental and physical anabolic state. This precise ratio of quality foods, along with other depression-busting nutrients such as omega-3 fatty acids and alpha lipoic acid, will balance out your body's chemistry, enhance your ability to burn fat, build muscle, and help your body release natural medicines such as serotonin and endorphins. Together, the *Feeling Good for Life* Exercise Solution and *Nutrition-4-Life* Diet will provide you with everything you need to know to begin exercising regularly, eat properly, and live life the way it is meant to be lived—healthy, strong, and depression free. Is there any other intervention that can make you feel great *and* get you in shape at the same time? Not so far, and this is what makes *Feeling Good for Life* so unique.

Would you believe that *Feeling Good for Life* costs less then a day's supply of Prozac or one session of psychotherapy? This new self-help therapy only needs to be used three days a week and will take up less then 1 percent of the time available to you during the day. Would you try *Feeling Good for Life* if you knew you would start feeling better within days of beginning your program? Well, if you're ready to make the decision to change your mind and body with *Feeling Good for Life*, you will not only be taking a step in the right direction, but a quantum leap in gaining control of your emotional and physical health forever.

Feeling Good for Life is divided into 5 chapters, each working synergistically to help you get in great shape and become depression free for life. Chapter 1 provides you with a questionnaire to assess your current emotional state and then goes on to discuss how researchers have used the powerful mood-elevating effects of exercise to help thousands of people conquer the blues. Chapters 2 and 3 discuss the different forms of exercise and guide you step-by-step in designing your own personalized *Feeling Good for Life* Exercise Solution. I have provided detailed instructions and illustrations for 7 aerobic exercises, 34 weight training exercises, and 9 stretching exercises to make certain that you have a variety of options to choose from during your *Feeling Good for Life* Exercise Solution. Chapter 4 shows you how to incorporate the *Nutrition-4-Life* Diet into your daily routine without turning your life upside down. It can be tough to change your eating habits and this is why I have provided easy-to-follow methods that show you how to adjust your lifestyle to begin eating healthy for the rest of your life. Chapter 5 provides you with a system of clinically proven techniques that will teach you how to access and utilize the power of self-motivation. I will show you how to use your own internal skills to help you become motivated and remain invested in working toward your exercise, nutrition, and mental health goals. I have also provided you with a 10-week *Feeling Good for Life* Journal in the back of this book to help you record your progress and stay on track. Lastly, I encourage you to visit *FeelingGoodforLife*.com. My site will provide you with online progress charts to help you keep track of your workouts, diet, as well as how you are feeling. The site also points you to numerous resources on exercise, nutrition, and mental health. This combination of powerful knowledge, consistent exercise, a specialized diet, and clinically tested motivational and adherence techniques makes up the *Feeling Good for Life* Experience and will give you the greatest chance of success in burning fat, building muscle, elevating your mood, and conquering depression.

Many of the people reading this book will approach this situation from the context of very personal struggles with the blues. You may have tried many other methods to improve your life, but have been disappointed. Some of you may approach the issue from a different perspective. Rather than personally struggling with feelings of deep sadness and gloom, you may be reaching out to a loved one or a close friend who is trying to cope with the blues. You may be a mental health professional seeking an innovative intervention that can soothe the pain of your clients suffering from longstanding feelings of depression. Others may simply be looking for a clear and authoritative guide on how to get in great shape by beginning to exercise regularly and eat healthy. Regardless of your reasons for reading this book, you can experience the powerful impact of the message that you have the power to change the way you are feeling by using your body. After reading only a few chapters, you will learn ways of releasing the powerful and miraculous self-cures that lie inside all of us. Within a matter of weeks, the sadness can move aside so that happiness can enter. Depression will subside so that euphoria can inhabit the mind and the body. The problem of depression, which seemed hopeless for so long, can now be treated by turning to the new, all natural mental health therapy—*Feeling Good for Life.*

Marcos Salazar

Taos, New Mexico

August 2001

CHAPTER I

Dispelling the Black Cloud with *Feeling Good for Life*™

Move Your Body, Move Your Mind

Think of the last time you felt sad and blue. What did you do to make yourself feel better? How long did it take you to get out of your slump? In all likelihood, you've resorted to various strategies when feeling down in the dumps. Maybe you went for a long drive and thought through the causes of your sadness or perhaps you wrote about your feelings in a journal. Maybe you turned to a loved one or even sought out professional help to talk through your feelings of hurt and despair. Perhaps you asked your physician for some medication that might take the edge off. Or quite possibly you did nothing at all because you simply felt incapable of taking any action. Your feelings may have left you so immobilized that the very thought of helping yourself seemed far too difficult. As a result, you waited it out, biding your time, hoping that the dark cloud of sadness would eventually fade from the sky of your world. And even long after your negative feelings subsided, you may have still found yourself fearful that such a dreaded experience might return, and your mind and body might once again be held prisoner by this emotional demon. If indeed you are feeling down or you live with agonizing fears of becoming depressed, you need not worry any longer. By using the principles in *Feeling Good for Life*, you will soon learn how to summon the power that lies within your own body to drive away the blues and prevent them from ever returning.

Taking this step is not beyond you. We all have the ability to enhance our mood and create a better life by using our bodies as vehicles to better mental and physical health. By harnessing the strength that lies within, you will learn how to heal yourself by utilizing your body's natural medicines. In a relatively short amount of time you can begin to derive benefits similar to those experienced by people participating in psychotherapy or taking antidepressant medication. Soon you will join the thousands of people who have turned to regular exercise and quality nutrition to elevate their mood and conquer depression. Imagine waking up in the morning a few weeks from now, looking in the mirror, and saying to yourself, "I feel great today!" Doesn't that sound terrific? By using *Feeling Good for Life,* you can make this a reality.

Depression—An Epidemic with No End in Sight

The first thing I want you to recognize is that if you are feeling blue, you are not alone—more than 19 million people suffer from depression each year. As startling as this figure is, some experts even believe that the real number is two to three times greater. Despite the fact that mental health professionals have devoted great amounts of time and effort in trying to understand the causes and best treatments for depression, this emotional plague has taken on a life of its own with the number of people who develop depression expanding each year. The World Health Organization predicts that by the year 2020, depression will be the most common health problem in the world and will become the second most common cause for disability and premature death. In addition to the tremendous emotional toll caused by depression, the economic impact it will have on our nation is alarming. Experts estimate that the cost will skyrocket to more than 50 billion dollars each year due to lost time, reduced productivity at work, and increased expenses in health care management.

Depression has become such a common part of our lives that many times it is difficult to recognize. People deeply troubled by feelings of intense sadness and gloom find it difficult to understand what's wrong with them, resulting in only a small percentage of depressed people seeking out professional help. Over two thirds of those who suffer from depression do not seek treatment for their problem, even when their depression is quite serious. A startling report by the National Depressive and Manic Depressive Association concluded that 55 percent of people with depression are neither diagnosed nor treated by their primary family physicians. The obstacles to seeking help are compounded by a health care system that is commonly unresponsive to the needs of depressed individuals. In fact, many people who turn to their managed care providers for referrals are discouraged from seeking help for their depression. This is a significant barrier to adequate mental health care.

If depression goes untreated, it can result in terrible tragedy. Each year tens of thousands of depressed people try to commit suicide, and more than 16,000 depressed people follow through by taking their own lives. Even children and adolescents, the precious future of our society, have turned out in increasing numbers to choosing an escape from emotional pain that involves the sacrifice of their own lives.

At the other end of the age continuum is a large population of aging people for whom depression and despair have become everyday struggles. Experts estimate that depression is a major cause and consequence of disability among the elderly, with up to one-fourth of nursing home residents suffering from depression. This serious mental health problem takes its toll on the elderly by dramatically increasing the likelihood of a downturn in physical health, eventually leading to premature death. As we look ahead to the change in the demographics of American society, we find that the aging baby boomers will join the elderly of America and encounter a multitude of mental health problems few will have anticipated. Even those who have been happy and well adjusted for decades may encounter incapacitating feelings of depression associated with failing health and other life disappointments. The cost of responding to this tremendous increase in the number of depressed people has not yet been calculated, but will certainly be felt by everyone in America.

Are you Depressed?

Although everyone feels down in the dumps from time to time, most people lack a clear sense of how such episodes compare to the experiences of other people. To assess how you are feeling, I have provided you with the *Goldberg Depression Inventory*, developed by Dr. Ivan Goldberg in appendix A. The *Goldberg Depression Inventory* is a reliable mood-measuring tool that assesses your current emotional state. You can also use the online version of this test by going to *www.psycom.net/depression.central.html* on Dr. Ivan Goldberg's Depression Central website.

Since the research on depression is so extensive, I have not included it in this chapter because I want to get you started with *Feeling Good for Life* as soon as possible. If you are interested in learning more about depression, I have included the major symptoms associated with depression in appendix A as well as numerous online and book resources in the appendix H.

Feeling Good for Life—The Exercise Solution to Depression

Over the past twenty years researchers around the world have consistently demonstrated that exercise produces powerful mood-elevating effects and improves depression just as well as psychotherapy and antidepressant medication. Although you may not be to entirely interested in understanding all the details of the studies that are about to be discussed, I want people to keep in mind that the information used to create *Feeling Good for Life* is based on sound scientific research. There are still many people, especially in the mental health care community, that do not know or believe that exercise is powerful enough to conquer depression. One of my goals in *Feeling Good for Life* is to remedy this situation by showing everyone that exercise has been rigorously tested and confirmed time and time again as one of the most effective and economically viable ways to elevate mood and combat depression.

Exercise Boosts Your Mood

The ancient Greeks were one of the first civilizations to recognize that a healthy body promotes a healthy mind. This anecdotal evidence was finally scientifically tested in the later part of the 20th century when researchers consistently verified the Greeks assumptions. In fact, by 1984 there were over 1,000 publications endorsing the mental health benefits of regular exercise and there have been thousands more since.

In one of the most well-controlled studies to investigate the impact of exercise on mood, Thomas DiLorenzo and his colleagues from the University of Missouri Columbia took 111 healthy adults without clinical depression and randomly assigned them to either an exercise or control group. At the beginning of the study, each participant received two psychological tests: the *Beck Depression Inventory* (BDI), which measures a person's current level of depressive symptoms, and the *Profile of Mood States* (POMS), which measures depression, anxiety, and vigor.

The participants in the exercise group were instructed to use a stationary bicycle for approximately 30 minutes, 3 to 4 times per week, for 12 weeks. The people in the control group were asked to refrain from beginning an exercise program or any other form of self-help therapy such as dieting or relaxation training during the study. At the end of the 12 weeks the investigators retested both groups using the same psychological instruments and found that the people who participated in the exercise program had significantly lowered their scores on these scales whereas the control group's scores remained the same.

Many other clinical trials have confirmed these results by demonstrating that exercise can dramatically improve our psychological well being. Dr. I. McCann and Dr. D. Holms took 43 college women with substantial mood problems that fell short of the criteria for clinical depression and assigned them to aerobic exercise, relaxation training, or a control group. At the end of 10 weeks, the people in the aerobic exercise group scored considerably lower on the depression inventories than the other two groups. Dr. D. Holmes later teamed up with Dr. D. Roth and conducted another study involving 55 non-depressed college students who had experienced a high number of stressful events over the past year. The students were assigned to an aerobic exercise, relaxation training, or control group. At the end of 11 weeks, those who participated in the exercise program had much lower scores on the depression scales compared to the other students.

Exercise Fights Depression

In one of the earliest studies examining the mood-elevating powers of exercise, Dr. Egil Martinsen and his colleagues gathered 49 clinically depressed patients and assigned them to either one of two groups. The exercise group was given an exercise prescription of either jogging or walking for 1 hour 3 times a week while the non-exercise group took part in occupational therapy that did not include any form of rigorous physical activity. This group served as a control group to make sure that any improvement in the exercise group was not due just to the passage of time.

At the initial evaluation, researchers administered the *Beck Depression Inventory* and found that there was no difference in the depression levels of both groups. The researchers then tested these patients after 9 weeks of either regular exercise or occupational therapy to see if there was any difference between the two groups and found that the patients in the exercise group had improved considerably. In fact, the depression scores dropped almost twice as much as the non-exercise group. Even more amazing is that these individuals reported feeling better almost as soon as they starting exercising.

Dr. Nalin Singh and his colleagues from Harvard Medical School investigated the impact that weight lifting had on depression in elderly people. Each subject in the study was given the *Beck Depression Inventory* and then randomly assigned to either a progressive resistance training program or a health education program for 10 weeks. The exercise group underwent a high-intensity progressive resistance training program 3 days a week while the control group engaged in an interaction health education program made up of lectures and videos, followed by a discussion twice a week for 1 hour. At the end of the study, the researchers found that the people who exercised regularly had improvements in their depression 2 to 3 times greater then those in the control group.

Exercise Compared to Psychotherapy

If exercise works so well at boosting our mood and improving depression, how does it match up to the traditional treatment of psychotherapy? Dr. John Greist was the first researcher to take a close look at this comparison by randomly assigning 28 outpatients with depression to either an exercise group that ran for over 40 minutes, 3 times a week, or one of two forms of individual psychotherapy. The results of Dr. Greist's study were quite surprising to the mental health community. At the end of 10 weeks the participants in *all* three groups showed significant reductions in depression. More importantly, there was no significant difference in improvement among the three groups. In other words, exercise worked just as well as psychotherapy. And people who kept exercising continued to show improvement at the 1, 3, 6, and 9-month follow-ups.

Michael Klein and his colleagues from Concordia University in Canada followed up this study by investigating the effects of exercise versus psychotherapy on 74 patients diagnosed with either major or minor depression. Each participant was randomly assigned to either a running, meditation and relaxation, or psychotherapy group. At the end of 12 weeks the researchers found a significant reduction in depression scores in each group, but again there was no real difference between exercise and psychotherapy. In fact, the follow-up study showed that the people who continued to exercise felt better than the people still using psychotherapy.

Exercise Just as Effective as Antidepressants

Antidepressants are currently the number one form of therapy for depression. Even though more and more antidepressants are being recommended each year, the rate of depression is reaching epic proportions and showing no sign of slowing down. More importantly, antidepressants can be expensive and carry unwanted side effects, such as dizziness, dry mouth, nausea, and sexual dysfunction. How does exercise compare to this dominant form of therapy?

To investigate this, James Blumenthal, Michael Babyak, and their colleagues from Duke University randomly assigned 156 men and women diagnosed with major depressive disorder to one of three groups: an aerobic exercise program, antidepressant medication, or a combination of exercise and medication. At the outset of the study researchers administered two depression assessment instruments, the *Hamilton Depression Scale* and the *Beck Depression Inventory*, and found that there was no difference in the level of depression among the three groups. Next, the subjects were assigned to each of their groups and monitored throughout the whole study. The subjects in the exercise group participated in 3 exercise sessions per week for 16 consecutive weeks. Each exercise session began with 10 minutes of warm-up exercise followed by 30 minutes of continuous walking or jogging at a moderate intensity, then concluded with 5 minutes of cool-down exercise. Subjects in the medication group received the medication Zoloft, a selective serotonin reuptake inhibitor (SSRI). Select serotonin reuptake inhibitors work by increasing the availability of serotonin in the brain, which is how they are believed to alleviate symptoms of depression. Zoloft was chosen because of its demonstrated effectiveness and relatively limited number of side effects. Subjects in the exercise/medication group received the same type of medication and performed the same exercise regimen as those in the two other groups.

At the end of 16 weeks the researchers found that the subjects in all three groups experienced reductions in depressive symptoms; however the most impressive finding was that there was no significant difference between exercise alone and the two other groups. Over 60 percent of those in the exercise group no longer met the diagnostic criteria for major depressive disorder, compared to 68 percent of the people in the medication group, and 65 percent of those in the exercise/medication group. In other words, exercise by itself was comparable to the effectiveness of antidepressant medication and comparable to medication combined with exercise in alleviating the subject's symptoms of depression. These findings are groundbreaking and are going to have a profound impact on the way we think about treating depression. Now, we can use exercise to reduce America's reliance on antidepressant medication and decrease the cost of treating this debilitating disorder.

Exercise Prevents Depression

Some people who are currently not afflicted with the blues may still have vivid memories of past depressive episodes that were troubling or incapacitating. If you are one of these individuals, *Feeling Good for Life* can serve a different function. Rather than turning to exercise in an effort to alleviate depression, you can use *Feeling Good for Life* as a preventive measure to ward off the return of distressing symptoms of the blues. Researchers have demonstrated that exercise has protective qualities powerful enough to keep this intruder from invading your life. In a study of Norwegian soldiers exposed to stressful life events, it was shown that soldiers who engaged in regular exercise were significantly less depressed 12 weeks after their exposure to the stressful life event compared to those who were sedentary.

Michael Babyak and his colleagues from Duke University tested how exercise compared to antidepressants in preventing people from falling back into their depressive states by conducting a 6-month follow-up study on the original patients who participated in the exercise versus antidepressant trial we discussed previously. When the researchers conducted the same psychological measurements 6 months after the initial study, they came up with some very surprising results. The researchers found that the subjects who continued to exercise were much less likely to see their depression return than the individuals who relied on medication alone or used a combination of both medication and exercise. In fact, only 8 percent of those in the exercise group relapsed, compared to 38 percent of those in the medication group, and 31 percent of those in the medication/exercise group. This means that 4 times as many people relapsed when they used antidepressants compared to people who used exercise alone! Clearly, regular exercise is a powerful tool in decreasing the likelihood of depression from ever returning and can sustain the positive psychological benefits you will experience during *Feeling Good for Life*.

You may be wondering how quickly you will start *Feeling Good for Life*. Well, this answer depends on a number of factors. Individual characteristics as well as the seriousness of a person's emotional state must be taken into account. However, research suggests that you can start deriving the mood-elevating benefits of exercise right from your first workout.

Dr. Fernando Dimeo and his colleagues demonstrated this fast acting antidepressant effect of exercise when they investigated how soon people's depression would improve after they began exercising. Twelve people diagnosed with moderate to severe depression were given an exercise prescription of walking on a treadmill for 30 minutes a day for 10 days. The researchers then measured how much their depression improved and found that their symptoms had dropped by an average of one third. In fact, 5 of the patients had their depression scores decrease by over 50 percent in only 10 days! Although this was a small study, exercise seems to have the power to produce a substantial improvement in mood in a very short amount of time. What is even more surprising is that exercise worked faster than antidepressant drugs, which generally take two to four weeks to begin working.

You may wonder if you need to exercise everyday to derive all the psychological benefits produced by exercise. Although some research has pointed to a relationship between increased physical fitness and improvements in mental health, exercising on a more casual basis has been shown to produce the mood-elevating benefits needed to drive away the blues. Studies indicate that low to moderate exercise 3 to 5 times a week is enough to help people feel psychologically sharper, less depressed, and generally more positive in their outlook on life.

How Does Exercise Boost Mood and Fight Depression?

The most unique quality of exercise is that it uses a dual antidepressant effect to improve your mental health. While antidepressants work through boosting vital neurotransmitters in your brain and psychotherapy improves your psychological health, exercise works by doing *both*. Exercise simulates your body's natural mood-elevating medicines as well as helps strengthen your mind psychologically to produce a physiological/psychological punch so strong it can conquer depression. This duel antidepressant effect is what makes exercise such a unique treatment and so far is the only intervention that combines two powerful therapies into one.

Boost Those Serotonin Levels

You have probably heard of serotonin from people talking about popular drugs such as Prozac and Zoloft. These medications known as Select Serotonin Reuptake Inhibitors (SSRIs) are used to treat a number of psychological conditions (including depression) by recycling low levels of serotonin. These medications accomplish this by blocking serotonin from being taken back up by the neuron it was released from, allowing more availability of serotonin inside the brain. Well, exercise solves this need to recycle low levels of serotonin by actually enhancing your ability to make new serotonin, resulting in an increase in the amount we produce in our brain. This increase in serotonin is made as a byproduct of one of the most beneficial qualities of exercise—the breakdown of fat.

Serotonin is created when the amino acid tryptophan gets transported from the bloodstream into the brain and is converted by a number of chemical reactions into serotonin. The influx of tryptophan into the brain dictates how much serotonin will be produced; therefore the more tryptophan that enters your brain, the more serotonin that is synthesized.

Tryptophan usually floats in the bloodstream with about 80 percent of it attached to a protein molecule called albumen. The rest of the tryptophan is in free form or unattached to any other molecule. This free form tryptophan is the kind that can readily pass from the blood into the brain and is the key to boosting serotonin levels. If you can get more free form tryptophan in the bloodstream, more can enter the brain to make serotonin.

So how does exercise use fat to increase serotonin levels? During your *Feeling Good for Life* Exercise Solution, you are going to use bodyfat for energy by breaking down fat into molecules called free fatty acids. A special property of these free fatty acids is that they like to compete with tryptophan to bind to albumen. So when you start burning fat during exercise, you will increase the amount of free fatty acids wanting to bind to albumin, which will cause less tryptophan to bind to albumin and automatically lead to an increase the amount of free form tryptophan in the blood. This is going to allow more tryptophan to pass into the brain to make more serotonin. So while you are trimming down your bodyfat during your *Feeling Good for Life* Exercise Solution, you will also be using your body as an antidepressant by boosting your serotonin levels.

Endorphins—The Natural High

One of the most widely used medications over the past century is the pain-relieving drug known as morphine. This naturally occurring alkaloid found in the opium poppy seed plant works by binding to receptors in our brain that regulate pain levels. Since morphine is a substance found outside the human body, it seems unusual that there are receptors for morphine to bind to inside our brain. This suggests that there must be some kind of opium-like compound that is produced within our own body that exerts a similar effect as morphine. There are such substances that bind to these same analgesic receptor sites—endorphins.

Whenever something from the external world hurts you, your body forms a natural defense by releasing endorphins to reduce the amount of pain you will feel. Although most times endorphins are released when you feel physical pain, studies suggest that endorphins can also play a role in emotional pain. People who are depressed tend to have lower levels of endorphins, possibly resulting in a weakened natural defense system that allows depression to wreak havoc in their lives. Fortunately, exercise can increase endorphin levels and give a boost to your defense system when it fights against the attacks from depression.

You have probably heard of the "runner's high" that people experience after an intense workout or in the home stretch of a marathon. This high is thought to be the result of endorphins being released into our body. Runners and other athletes say that it is this euphoric feeling produced by endorphins that has allowed them to break through the physical and mental barriers that have limited them in achieving their fitness goals, resulting in better performance and increased confidence in their abilities. This same type of process may be what is causing you to feel great after a good, hard workout. So each time you exercise, think of it as though you are giving yourself a shot of "natural" morphine that will help you feel calmer, more relaxed, and less depressed after you exercise.

Exercise Thermogenesis

One of the major physiological processes our body goes through during exercise is an increase in core body temperature. We call this physiological process *exercise thermogenesis*. While working out, your body begins to utilize and burn more energy, producing an elevation in body heat. This "warming up" of the body prepares your muscles for exercise and results in improved performance and a decrease in the likelihood of injury. And the more you exercise, the more your body temperature continues to rise. This elevation in core body temperature is thought to be what produces the decrease in tension and anxiety we experience during exercise.

Elevating body temperature to produce a therapeutic effect dates back thousands of years when people used to travel to soak in hot mineral-laden waters to achieve alleged health benefits and a better sense of well-being. Today, people still practice this form of therapy by soaking in hot tubs or using sauna baths. Studies have shown that exposing yourself to these types of high temperatures relieves muscle tension and decreases anxiety. Exercise may produce this same type of thermogenic effect, producing the elevation in mood and decrease in depressive feelings you feel after a good workout.

Another theory that supports the exercise thermogenic hypothesis is that exercise may have a similar healing effect as developing a fever. Whenever your body is invaded by bacteria or viruses and becomes sick, it responds to these intruders by releasing chemicals called endogenous pyrogens. These pyrogen molecules react to foreign invaders by causing your body temperature to rise, sending your body into an alarm state. This alarm sets off a cascade of physiological reactions that prepares your body to fend off foreign invaders. This same fever-like experience may occur during exercise. When your body temperature rises as you workout, it may send out signals to your brain telling it to release certain chemicals that prime your natural bodily defenses to fight off emotional intruders such as anxiety, stress, and depression.

A Strong Body Equals a Strong Mind

In addition to the multitude of physiological improvements, exercise will also make you psychologically stronger. Each time you go out and exercise, you will be disciplining yourself, providing the opportunity to begin taking control of your mind by taking control of your body. Your feelings of self-worth will improve because you will be assuming responsibility for your health by taking the initiative to improve your current emotional state.

You will also notice that once you begin *Feeling Good for Life*, you will have increased energy. Things that used to tire you out will seem much easier to accomplish. You will feel more alert and be able to concentrate better at work, home, and play. You are also going to change how your body looks by building muscle and burning fat during your *Feeling Good for Life* Exercise Solution. This is going to help you get that well-defined physique you always wanted, which will improve your self-image and help you gain back your self-esteem and self-confidence.

For most of you who start *Feeling Good for Life*, regular exercising will be something new. To make sure you get off to the right start, I have provided detailed instructions on everything you need to know to incorporate exercise into your life. After a couple of workouts you will begin to get the hang of things and exercising will seem second nature. Your form will become smoother, you will be able to exercise for longer periods of time, and you will be able to lift more weight. This mastery of your *Feeling Good for Life* Exercise Solution will improve your self-efficacy—your ability to control and master things in your life. As you gain better control of this aspect of your life, these positive feeling will soon proliferate and flow into other areas causing you to have a much more positive outlook on the world.

Exercise also helps us psychologically by serving as a way of escaping the toils and pressures we face in our stressful lives. Money, work, or the loss of an important relationship can certainly affect our emotionally state.

These stresses can bring us down emotionally, especially when we are dealing with more than one issue at a time. For this reason, exercise can serve as a way of taking a time-out from the parts of our lives that can cause us to feel blue. You can escape by taking a long bike ride along the countryside, wake up early for a morning run, or go to the gym to exercise your stress out. When you exercise, you can focus on how your body feels as it moves, how you are breathing, or how fast your heart is beating. This will make you become more in tune with your body and interrupt the constant thinking and focusing on the problems in your life.

Let the Journey Begin

In this chapter you learned that you have the power to change how you feel by using your body as a vehicle to attain all your mental and physical health goals. Now it's time to start learning how you can utilize this valuable research and apply it to your own life. In the following chapters we will draw a road map for you to begin burning fat, building muscle, boosting your mood, and conquering depression by using *Feeling Good for Life*. Let's get started.

CHAPTER 2

The *Feeling Good for Life* Aerobic Solution

Overcome the Inertia and You Will Climb Out of the Abyss

The first chapter gave you the knowledge to change your life forever. This chapter will help you start turning this knowledge into action by showing you how to apply this powerful research to your own life. In the next two chapters I am going to guide you step-by-step in designing your personal *Feeling Good for Life* Exercise Solution. As you will soon see, the *Feeling Good for Life* Exercise Solution is one of the easiest and most time-efficient ways to improve your mental and physical health. You will only have to begin using your *Feeling Good for Life* Exercise Solution for 20–30 minutes a day, 3–4 times per week to receive all the amazing benefits that come from regular exercise. Can you believe that this amounts to less than 1 percent of the time available to you each day? It is not necessary for you to turn your life upside down to receive all the body-shaping, mood-boosting benefits of *Feeling Good for Life*.

Is Exercise Safe for You?

Before you begin any of the *Feeling Good for Life* Exercise Solutions, it is necessary to determine if increasing your physical activity is safe for you. Because the primary purpose of *Feeling Good for Life* is to improve the quality of your life, it would be counter productive if you aggravated an existing medical condition by exercising. Therefore, it is a good idea to take some necessary precautions before you begin using your *Feeling Good for Life* Exercise Solution.

Some people may wonder whether they should see a doctor before increasing their physical activity. For most people this is not necessary. The *Feeling Good for Life* Exercise Solution is a safe activity that involves little risk to a person's health; however, in some specific cases it is a good idea to check with a doctor before beginning *Feeling Good for Life*. The American College of Sports Medicine (1995) recommends that if you have cardiac, pulmonary, or metabolic problems or are over the age of 40 (50 for women), you should have a pre-exercise exam by your physician. This may seem time consuming and unnecessary, but it is necessary to insure your safety.

Because some people have other health concerns, such as arthritis, osteoporosis, hypertension, coronary heart disease, or diabetes, I have provided *Feeling Good for Life* Training Guidelines for these special populations in appendix C. If you are diagnosed with any of these illnesses, you can use these recommendations to tailor your *Feeling Good for Life* Exercise Solution; however, it is still a good idea to check with your physician to make sure that you do not aggravate your current condition. If you are currently taking any medication for your depression, consult your mental health care professional to see if starting *Feeling Good for Life* will benefit you in addition to your current treatment.

If you are concerned about the cost of a medical examination or are not sure you are at risk, completing the *Feeling Good for Life* Readiness Questionnaire will provide you with an inexpensive and simple way to determine if you need a health screening. Please read the questions carefully for they will tell you whether you are healthy enough to participate in the regimens outlined in *Feeling Good for Life*.

Feeling Good for Life Readiness Questionnaire

YES NO   1. Are you on antidepressant medication that may have side effects that could interfere with increasing your physical activity?

YES NO   2. Are you over the age of 65 or not accustomed to exercise?

YES NO   3. Are you a diabetic?

YES NO   4. If you have diabetes, are you currently taking any medication that may interfere with increasing your physical activity?

YES NO   5. Do you have a bone or joint problems such as arthritis or osteoporosis that could be worse by increasing your physical activity?

YES NO   6. Has your doctor ever informed you that you have heart problems?

YES NO   7. Do you commonly have chest pain when you do physical activity?

YES NO   8. In the past month, have you had chest pain when you were not doing physical activity?

YES NO   9. Do you often feel faint or have spells of severe dizziness?

YES NO   10. Has your doctor told you your blood pressure is too high?

YES NO   11. Is your doctor currently prescribing drugs that affect you blood pressure or an existing heart condition?

YES NO   12. Is there a good physical reason not mentioned above why you should not increase your physical activity?

If you have answered yes to one or more of the questions, you may be endangering your health by participating in one of the *Feeling Good for Life* Exercise Solutions. Consult a physician and obtain his or her permission before beginning one of the exercise programs outlined in this book. When you are at the doctor's office, discuss what form of exercise you plan to undertake and ask for recommendations on what type of physical activity she thinks is best for you. If you have answered no to all the questions in the *Feeling Good for Life* Readiness Questionnaire, then you are ready to move on to the rest of the chapter and begin designing you own personal *Feeling Good for Life* Exercise Solution.

The Two *Feeling Good for Life* Exercise Solutions

There are two *Feeling Good for Life* Exercise Solutions that I have created for you: the *Feeling Good for Life* Aerobic Solution and the *Feeling Good for Life* Weight Training Solution. The *Feeling Good for Life* Aerobic Solution, which is the focus of the rest of this chapter, is divided into a number of *Feeling Good for Life* Exercise Solutions so you can have a variety of options to choose from to help you begin burning fat to boost your serotonin levels. In chapter 3 you will learn how to design your own personal *Feeling Good for Life* Weight Training Solution, which will consist of a specialized 10-week program that will provide you with a foundation in helping you decrease bodyfat and build muscle. Chapter 3 also includes three Advanced *Feeling Good for Life* Weight Training Solutions structured around specific fitness goals you may have such as improving muscular endurance, accelerating fat loss, or enhancing muscle growth.

Which *Feeling Good for Life* Exercise Solution is More Effective?

Is one *Feeling Good for Life* Exercise Solution better than the other in elevating mood and fighting depression? Dr. Harold Sexton and his colleagues from Innherred Hospital in Levanger, Norway, set out to answer this question by taking 52 depressed patients and randomly assigning them to either a walking or jogging program. Each group exercised for 30 minutes, 3 to 4 times a week, for 8 weeks. At the end of study, the researched discovered that both groups had recovered from depression and more importantly, found no significant difference between those who walked or jogged.

In order to test the difference between aerobic exercise and weight training in alleviating symptoms of depression, Elizabeth Doyne and Deborah Ossip-Klein from the University of Rochester randomly assigned 40 participants with clinical depression to a running group, weight training group, or control group. People in the aerobic exercise group walked or ran around a track for over 35 minutes, 3 times a week while subjects in the weight training group performed a full body workout consisting of 10 weight training exercises. At the end of 12 weeks, subjects in both exercise groups were no longer clinically depressed; however, the major finding was that there was no difference between the two exercising groups—both running and weight training produced an equally effective antidepressant effect.

Now which *Feeling Good for Life* Exercise Solution is best for you? That is what I will be helping you decide in the next two chapters. A combination of the two will give you the most physical improvements, but for now it is more important that you focus on performing only one *Feeling Good for Life* Exercise Solution. This way you do not overwhelm yourself at the start of your program.

As you read about the different *Feeling Good for Life* Exercise Solutions, you will probably notice that different aspects of each program will appeal to you. If you are not sure about which one you should use, try one out and if you do not like it, you always have the option to switch to another one. You certainly don't want to spend any part of your day doing something that is not fun. The important thing here is to find the *Feeling Good for Life* Exercise Solution that you enjoy and feel comfortable performing.

The 10-Week *Feeling Good for Life* Aerobic Solution

As chapter 1 demonstrated, aerobic exercise is extremely effective in improving your mood and fighting depression. But in addition to all the psychological benefits you will gain from your *Feeling Good for Life* Aerobic Solution, you will also experience countless physical benefits. One of the main reasons that people begin exercising is they want to lose weight and the *Feeling Good for Life* Aerobic Solution is one of the best activities you can use to accomplish this. During aerobic exercise your body burns fat for energy and as you become more aerobically fit, your body will become even better at breaking down fat to use for fuel during exercise. This decrease in bodyfat not only gives you a leaner looking body, but also boosts serotonin levels and safeguards you against many of the problems associated with being overweight.

Aerobic exercise also has a profound impact on your heart and circulatory system. As you get in better shape, your heart becomes much more efficient at pumping blood throughout your body, reducing your resting heart rate and increasing the amount of blood your heart pumps out with each beat. Another major benefit of aerobic exercise is that it increases the strength of your bones, tendons, and ligaments, which helps alleviate many of the health problems associated with old age. Lastly, your *Feeling Good for Life* Aerobic Solution will reduce the risk of chronic illness, such as coronary heart disease, osteoporosis, and diabetes.

How Hard Should You Exercise?

How intense should your workouts be? The American College of Sports Medicine (1995) recommends that you stay within the range of 60–85 percent of your maximum heart rate. How do you determine your maximum heart rate? The most convenient way is to use the age predicted maximum heart method, which uses the 220-minus-age formula. You can calculate your max heart rate by using the following equation:

Training Heart Rate = Maximal Predicted Heart Rate (220–age) x Desired Percent of Maximal Heart Rate (60–85)

For example, a 40-year-old woman who wants to exercise in the 60–70 percent range of her maximal heart rate would perform the following equation:

220 – 40 (age) = 180 (Predicted Max Heart Rate)
180 x .60 (60 Percent Exercise Intensity) = 108 Exercise Heart Rate
180 x .70 (70 Percent Exercise Intensity) = 126 Exercise Heart Rate

From the results of the calculation, this woman should exercise at an intensity within the range of 108–126 beats per minute. You can check your heart rate while exercising by putting your fingers (not your thumb) on the side of your neck or on the front of your wrist for about 15 seconds and then multiply that number by 4. If you are exercising below 60 percent of your maximal heart rate, you will want to pick up the pace of your workout and if you are exercising close to 85 percent of your maximal heart rate, you may want to lower your exercise intensity. A good rule of thumb is to start at the lower range, about 60–75 percent of your maximum heart rate, and then gradually work your way up to a higher intensity.

You can also utilize another simple method of measuring how hard you are exercising by using a 1-to-10 self-intensity scale. For example, you can think of level 1 as sitting on the couch watching TV, while level 2 might be going to get something from the refrigerator, whereas level 10 would be running as hard as you can or maxing out on the amount of weight you can lift, i.e., 100 percent exertion. In terms of exercising, level 4 or 5 would be an appropriate place to start. You can think of level 5 as mild/moderate intensity. So when you begin exercising, start out slowly and as you become more physically fit, gradually work up to a higher intensity level.

When is the Best Time to Exercise?

Is there a best time to exercise? The answer to the question is yes—whenever it is most convenient for you. One of the main goals of *Feeling Good for Life* is to get you to make exercise a regular part of your life, so whenever you find it easiest to exercise, set that time aside to work out and do nothing else.

Many people enjoy exercising before their first meal of the day. There are many advantages to exercising in the morning. Research shows that you burn a greater percentage of fat (up to 50 percent more) if you conduct aerobic exercise in the morning. Also, if you exercise first thing in the morning, you can accomplish one of your main goals at the start of the day.

For other people, mornings may be hectic and working out at the end of the day may fit into your schedule better. This, too, has its advantages. Exercising after a hard day's work can help cleanse the mind and relieve stress from the problems experienced throughout the day.

It is not a good idea to exercise after a large meal. After you eat, your body diverts a large supply of blood to your digestive system, which can interfere with the transport of extra blood needed for the muscles you will be using during exercise. This can cause great discomfort and increases the chances of cramping up. Also, as you will learn in the *Nutrition-4-Life* chapter, eating a large amount of carbohydrates before aerobic exercise will prevent you from burning bodyfat during your workout. So try to eat a small meal with low amounts of carbohydrates about 2 hours before you exercise.

Don't Forget to Warm-Up and Cool-Down

Including a warm-up and cool-down session is an essential part of your *Feeling Good for Life* Exercise Solution. These components often get overlooked, and without them you make yourself susceptible to unnecessary muscle soreness and injury. By dedicating a small portion of your workout to warming up and cooling down, you can ensure that you will have a safe and effective workout.

You can think of warming up your body as being similar to warming up your car on a winter morning. You cannot expect to start your car and have it instantly perform at its best. The car needs time to heat up and get things going. You cannot begin driving at full speed, so you have to start out slowly to avoid overloading the engine. Well, this is the same thing you have to do with your body when you are about to start exercising. Think of your muscles as your car's engine. By starting out slowly, you will gradually increase your heart rate and oxygen consumption, elevate your temperature, and get blood flowing throughout your body, ensuring that your muscles will be ready for the workout ahead. A good warm-up consists of low intensity aerobic work such as walking or slow tempo rhythmic callisthenic movements for about 5–7 minutes.

You should also include at least 5–7 minutes of cool-down to decrease your heart rate and overall metabolism after exercise. This reduces the possibility of post-exercise dizziness or fainting. It also aids in preventing delayed muscle stiffness you may feel after exercise. Low-level aerobic work similar to the warm-up should be performed.

Stretching it Out

Our bodies were designed to move thorough a wide range of motion and if we do not take our bodies through a variety of movements, they can become stiff and cause us unnecessary aches and pains. This is why stretching is such a vital component in physical fitness and overall health. By stretching regularly, you will provide your body with numerous benefits, such as increased flexibility and elasticity of your muscles, loosening up of the joints, increased neuromuscular coordination, improved muscular balance, and a decrease in muscle soreness after workouts. By incorporating a stretching routine into your *Feeling Good for Life* Exercise Solution, you will be utilizing all of your body's resources to improve your mental and physical health.

The best time to stretch your muscles is after your warm-up, during your cool-down, or between sets while weight training. It is never a good idea to stretch your muscles without warming up first because you will be putting unnecessary stress on your ligaments and tendons. When you are stretching, do not bounce or lock your joints. You want to hold each stretch for 15–30 seconds, relax, and repeat. To maximize the benefits of stretching, you may want to stretch the muscles that you are going to use or just have used for a longer period of time. Appendix B lists 9 great stretching exercises that will improve the flexibility of all your major muscle groups. Refer to the photos to make sure that you are performing each of the stretches properly.

Overtraining

One of the most common mistakes people make when they start working out is exercising too hard or too often. This is understandable because people can be highly motivated to start exercising and see results as soon as possible. However, before you decide to go out and exercise every day for hours at a time, let me remind you that all you need to do is exercise 20–30 minutes a day, 3 times a week to gain all the benefits we have discussed. You can eventually exercise more often, but for now I want you to focus on starting out slowly so you do not burn yourself out right from the start.

You see, when you exercise too hard or too often, it can lead to what sports doctors call overtraining. One of the major reasons people enter the state of overtraining is because they adopt the wrong mindset toward exercise. In general, most people view their lives in terms of quantity, ascribing to the economic principle of "more is better," and tend to pursue their aspirations in the same manner. When it comes to exercise, this mindset is a mistake and should be avoided. By this rational, you should work out longer and more often to get the most out of exercising. Think about that reasoning for a moment: If more is better, when should you stop exercising? At one hour, two hours, five hours? Soon you would have to be training all day to derive the benefits of exercise. Doesn't something sound wrong here?

If you were to believe that this is what you need to do to improve your mental health, you would be heading down a dark path that would cause you to lose energy, break down muscle, increase the risk of infection, and, worst of all, slip right back into the emotional abyss that you were trying to get out of. Research shows that overtraining has the potential to worsen your symptoms of depression, dragging you right back to where you started. Since this is the last thing you want to do, try to make the conscious effort not to train too much. If you don't heed this advice, the end result may be exactly the opposite of what you are trying to accomplish with *Feeling Good for Life*.

If by chance you do overtrain, the only treatment is to stop exercising and get some rest. Relax for a few days and refrain from exercise so you can allow your body to recover. It may sound a bit frightening that exercise can cause this, but there is little need to worry about overtraining during your *Feeling Good for Life* Experience. If you follow the workouts I have outlined in this chapter, your chances of overtraining are literally nonexistent. This is because the *Feeling Good for Life* Exercise Solutions will allow your body enough time to recover in between workouts, eliminating your chances of overtraining.

Delayed Onset Muscle Soreness

Delayed onset muscle soreness refers to the muscle soreness you usually feel about 24 to 48 hours after you exercise. It is completely natural for you to experience a little soreness after your workouts, especially at the beginning of the program, because your body is unaccustomed to the stress of exercise. As you continue to exercise on a more regular basis, your body will soon adapt and eventually become less sore after each workout.

Many people feel that soreness is a good indicator of whether they had a good workout the day before. This popular "cause and effect" idea is not

entirely accurate and should be avoided. Just because you did not feel sore
the day after your workout does not mean that you didn't work hard during your exercise session. Your lack of soreness simply indicates that your
body has adapted and become better at handling the stress of exercise. If
you keep trying to use soreness as an indicator of how effective your workouts are, you will soon have to exercise at an extremely high intensity or
for a prolonged period of time, which is going to lead to overtraining. And
when you start overtraining you are actually going to become consistently
sore because your body cannot fully recover from your workouts. If this
happens, take a few days off and then start back up again, slowly building
up your fitness level.

To help decrease muscle soreness, make sure to begin your *Feeling Good
for Life* Exercise Solution slowly and progress gradually. You should avoid
maximal lifting or all out running or cycling. As we discussed before,
stretching can reduce muscle soreness so try to stretch before, during, or
after you exercise.

Testing Your Fitness Level

Before you begin your *Feeling Good for Life* Aerobic Solution, you will
need to find out what your current fitness level is. You never want to start
out exercising too hard or too often and this is why I recommend that you
perform a walk test to determine how physically fit you are. How long you
can walk at a brisk pace without serious difficulty or fatigue will determine
at what level you should begin your *Feeling Good for Life* Aerobic Solution.

Get a timer and go for a brisk walk. Pay special attention to how long it
takes you to become a bit winded. Your pace should be faster then your normal walk, but not so fast that you are jogging. If you can walk for more than
5 minutes, but less then 10 minutes without becoming winded, it would be
best if you start at week 1 of the *Feeling Good for Life* Walking or Cycling
Solution. If you can walk for the full 10 minutes without becoming tired,

you can start at week 3 of the *Feeling Good for Life* Walking or Cycling Solution or week 1 of the *Feeling Good for Life* Jogging/Running Solution.

You may feel like you can exercise longer or more often, but before you do so, keep in mind that one of the main principles of the *Feeling Good for Life* Exercise Solution is progressive improvement. If you start out at too high an intensity or exercise for hours at a time, you will soon become sore, tired, and frustrated, which will decrease your chances of sticking to your *Feeling Good for Life* Exercise Solution. You must allow your body time to adapt to this new stress on your body before you decide to train harder and longer.

The *Feeling Good for Life* Walking Solution

We will begin with walking because it is a form of exercise that can be done by nearly everyone and performed almost anywhere. Walking has become very popular because it doesn't cost much money to get started, has a low rate of injury, and can be done at any time and in almost any type of weather. It is especially great for people who are not in good shape and want to start out slowly.

The Proper Walking Technique

When people go for a walk, most don't pay much attention to their form. However, there is a proper walking technique that should be followed to reduce the chances of injury while you exercise. Improper form will not put you in any immediate danger, but over the long run you will be putting your body under chronic stress that could eventually lead to a serious injury. To make sure that your walking program is safe and effective, it is necessary that you pay special attention to your walking form.

The first thing you should do is take a close look at your posture. Are you walking upright and not bending too much forward? An upright stance will conserve energy and decrease the risk of developing any lower back or neck problems. Your back should be straight, chest out, shoulders relaxed, and head up so you can focus on what is ahead of you. While walking, keep your arms bent and swing your arms past your hips, but not so much that your arms rise above your chest. Arm swinging should be kept to a minimum during walking and should only increase with speed.

One of the major problems that people encounter while trying to perform the right walking technique is using the proper foot strike. Many people assume that they should be walking on the balls of their feet. This type of foot strike may be appropriate for running, but it is inappropriate for walking and could result in foot problems if not corrected. The best technique for walking is the heel-to-toe foot strike. When your foot is landing, you should be lightly stepping on your heel, then roll your foot forward, eventually pushing off on the balls of your feet. A good way to make sure that you are using the proper foot strike is to check your shoes. After several weeks of walking if your shoes show more wear on the outer border of the heel than the rest of the shoe, then you are performing the proper walking technique.

Where Should You Walk?

This decision is a matter of personal choice, but you can pretty much exercise wherever you please. You can take a walk in your neighborhood, in the park, or in the streets on your lunch break. After a few weeks of training, you may want to go down some back roads and trails located around your neighborhood. It is nice to vary your route every so often and change things a little to keep boredom away and help maintain your interest.

What if the weather is too inclement for you to walk outside? You can remedy this problem by going to the local school gym or YMCA. If you live in a city, a great place to go walking is the mall. Most of these places open their buildings for "mall walkers" who walk in the morning before the stores open. These indoor buildings should give you enough back-up options in case the weather does not permit you to walk outdoors.

What Should You Wear?

The most important type of clothing that will ensure you enjoy your *Feeling Good for Life* Walking Solution is a comfortable pair of shoes. Because a good pair of shoes is so important, do not economize when purchasing footwear. If possible, try to invest in a good pair of shoes by going to a reputable sporting goods store and asking the advice of a salesperson. There are many different shoes made for numerous sporting activities (hiking shoes, running shoes, basketball shoes). Make sure that you get a walking shoe or a shoe that can be used for your specific activity. It is necessary to get a shoe with good arch supports, a firm, thick sole, and a padded heel. The sole should be very flexible because you bend your feet a great deal when you walk. It is also good to make sure that you have a good heel counter because your heels bare most of the weight when you are walking. A good pair of shoes will help you avoid foot, ankle, and lower back problems, as well as prevent blisters or calluses.

It is not necessary to wear fancy clothing while you are walking. However, I have some recommendations in case you decide to (or have to) walk in hot or very cold weather. Loose fitting nylon or cotton gym shorts and a T-shirt should be adequate for the summer or in warm climates. What you want in this type of whether is light, breathable clothing that you can move in. During the winter months or in cold climates, a sweatshirt or a jogging suit will do the job. It is better to wear several layers of light apparel than a single heavy garment because it is easier to move in. It is also a good idea to wear gloves and a hat. These articles of clothing are important because you can lose a great deal of body heat from your head and hands. When it becomes very cold and the temperature falls below 20 degrees Fahrenheit, it may be necessary to wear long underwear or tights. If you can afford it, invest in polypropylene garments that wick perspiration and keep you warm while exercising.

The Weekly *Feeling Good for Life* Walking Solution

Depending on how you did on the walk test, you are either going to begin exercising at week 1 or week 3 of the *Feeling Good for Life* Walking Solution. You are going to workout 3 times per week, gradually increasing the duration each week as you become more physically fit. Once you get to 35–40 minutes, it is not necessary to continue to increase the length of your workout. What you should be focusing on is increasing the intensity. By using this type of training, you will continue to become more fit, save time and burn more fat.

Your 10-Week *Feeling Good for Life* Walking Solution Schedule

	Monday	Tuesday	Wednesday	Thursday	Friday	Sat/Sun
Week 1	15 min		15 min		20 min	
Week 2	20 min		20 min		20 min	
Week 3	20 min		20 min		25 min	
Week 4	25 min		25 min		30 min	
Week 5	30 min		30 min		30 min	
Week 6	30min		30 min		35 min	20 min
Week 7	35 min		35 min		35 min	20 min
Week 8	35 min		35 min		35 min	25 min
Week 9	35 min		40 min		40 min	25 min
Week 10	40 min		40 min		40 min	30 min

The *Feeling Good for Life* Jogging/Running Solution

Jogging and running require the same type of movements as walking, but the intensity and quickness of the movements are much greater. The only real difference between jogging and running is that running is jogging but at a faster pace. Both are uncomplicated activities that can be done almost anywhere. However, even though jogging and running can be enjoyable activities, they are not for everyone. When you jog or run you are putting more stress on your knees, hips, and ankles because of the constant pounding when your feet hit the ground. Jogging and running offer many advantages, such as easy accessibility and a greater improvement in physical health in a shorter period of time. But if you don't believe that you are built to run, this type of exercise may not be the one for you. However, this will not prevent you from deriving all the physical and mental health benefits from the other *Feeling Good for Life* Aerobic Solutions in this chapter.

The Proper Jogging/Running Technique

The proper technique for jogging and running is similar to walking, with some slight modifications. When you pick up the pace, begin leaning your body slightly forward and lift your knees a little higher. Push off the balls of your feet more and move your arms a bit more vigorously. Make sure to keep your head up and not to hold your breath.

Your *Feeling Good for Life* Weekly Jogging/Running Solution

If you have been inactive for the past six months, make sure to start out at week 1 to allow your body enough time to adapt. This will give you the time to start out slowly and build up your fitness level until you are finally ready to begin the *Feeling Good for Life* Jogging/Running Solution.

Your *Feeling Good for Life* Jogging/Running Schedule

	Monday	Tuesday	Wednesday	Thursday	Friday	Sat/Sun
Week 1	25min Walking		25min Walking		25min Walking	
Week 2	30min Walking		30min Walking		30min Walking	
Week 3	Walk 5min Jog 10min		Walk 5min Jog 10min		Walk 5min Jog 10min	
Week 4	Walk 5min Jog 12min		Walk 5min Jog 12min		Walk 5min Jog 12min	
Week 5	Walk 5min Jog 14min		Walk 5min Jog 14min		Walk 5min Jog 14min	
Week 6	Walk 5min Jog 16min		Walk 5min Jog 16min		Walk 5min Jog 16min	
Week 7	Walk 2min Jog 18min		Walk 2min Jog 18min		Walk 2min Jog 18min	Walk 2min Jog 15min
Week 8	Walk 2min Jog 20min		Walk 2min Jog 20min		Walk 2min Jog 20min	Walk 2min Jog 16min
Week 9	Run 2min Jog 20min		Run 2min Jog 20min		Run 2min Jog 20min	Walk 2min Jog 17min
Week 10	Run 4min Jog 20min		Run 4min Jog 20min		Run 4min Jog 20min	Walk 2min Jog 18min

The *Feeling Good for Life* Cycling Solution

Cycling is one of the best forms of aerobic exercise and provides virtually all the same benefits as walking, jogging, and running. It is a good alternative for those who do not like to jog or run because it is low impact and is a minimal weight-bearing activity that puts little stress on your joints. There are two types of cycling you can use—indoor cycling on a stationary bike and outdoor cycling. Each has its advantages and disadvantages, but both provide you with the mental and physical benefits we have discussed. Use the same schedule as the 10-Week *Feeling Good for Life* Walking Solution.

Indoor Cycling

There are two types of stationary bikes found in most health clubs and fitness centers that you can use during you indoor *Feeling Good for Life* Cycling Solution—those that are upright like a traditional bicycle and ones that you sit down in. There is little difference between the two in their ability to give you a good workout, so you should choose the one that feels most comfortable to you. Most stationary bikes are electronically powered and have a digital display that gives you the ability to set the minutes and speed you want to work out at. When you are ready to begin, get on the bike, adjust the seat to a comfortable level where one leg is almost fully extended and the other has a slight bend in it, and begin peddling.

Outdoor Cycling

Bicycling outdoors can be extremely gratifying because you are outside with sunlight, fresh air, and varied landscape and scenery. You can go for a ride around your neighborhood, on some back trails around your area, or even to work. The disadvantages of this form of cycling is that it is highly dependent on the weather, should be done during the day, and may be unsafe in some city environments. By using the following recommendations you can get the most out of your outdoor *Feeling Good for Life* Cycling Solution.

1) Make sure to use a bicycle that has 10 speeds so that you can easily adapt to the different types of terrain that you will encounter.
2) Adjust the seat so that the leg on the down stroke is not completely extended. You should bend your torso so that it is bent slightly forward and your hands are placed firmly on the handlebars.
3) Keep your shoulders relaxed and elbows bent at all times.
4) Make sure that your wrists are not bent forward or backward excessively.
5) Always wear a cycling helmet when riding.
6) Take a water bottle with you.
7) Be aware of your surroundings and watch out for street signs and cars.

Feeling Good for Life Aerobic Solution Options

Today most health clubs offer a wide assortment of aerobic exercise machines. Although there have been no studies to date using these machines in testing the mood-elevating antidepressant effect of exercise, these machines produce the same physiological response as all the other exercises I have outlined here. Therefore, it would be perfectly fine to use them as an alternative during your *Feeling Good for Life* Aerobic Solution. You can use these machines in case you ever get bored or would like to add a little variety to your program. Simply follow the routine outlined for the *Feeling Good for Life* Walking Solution.

The Treadmill

The treadmill is a simple piece of exercise equipment in which a motorized belt allows you to walk or run in place. This machine has become very popular for a number of reasons. First, it is a convenient way for people to go for walks or runs if the whether is bad or if they live in a city where it may be too dangerous to walk on the streets. Secondly, treadmills are now designed well enough to absorb a great deal of the shock that your knees and ankles take from walking. Lastly, treadmills can move slowly enough to accommodate even the most out of shape person.

When you get on the treadmill, simply enter in the speed at which you want to walk or run and press start. The belt below your feet will begin moving and you just keep up with the pace you have set. There is also a button that will allow you to raise the bottom part of the treadmill to replicate the feeling of walking on an incline.

Make sure you start out slow and build up to your desired speed. Do not rely on the handrails for support. They can be used at the start of your program for balancing yourself when you are learning how to use the machine, but as soon as you feel comfortable, you should let go. If you have to use them, it means that you are going too fast and you should slow down.

Stairclimber

The purpose of the stairclimber is to mimic the movement of climbing without causing serious wear and tear on your joints like you would if you jogged up a flight of stairs or bleachers. It is important that you use good form with these machines. So many times people clutch onto the handrails or lean over the machines so they can move their feet faster. What they do not realize is that when they do this, they transfer the weight from their legs to their arms or the machine and reduce the effectiveness of their workout. When you are at the machine, place one foot on each of the pedals and begin moving your legs up and down in a stair-walking motion. At first you may have to use your hands to keep your balance, but once you have gotten the feeling of the machine only allow your fingertips to rest on the bars.

Elliptical Trainer and Precor

These are relatively new pieces of equipment that have become extremely popular in health clubs because of their unique range of motion. The elliptical and precor machines have two large pedals that follow the path of a stretched out oval, i.e. the shape of an ellipse. The motion feels like a combination of walking, stairclimber, and cross-country skiing.

When you are facing the machine, put your feet on the pedals, push forward, and follow the movement of the machine. You do not have to worry too much about your form other than not hugging the machine, because your feet will automatically follow the range of motion. Sometimes these machines have handles on each side to give you the option of also working your arms.

The *Feeling Good for Life* Interval Training Solution

After you finish the 10-Week *Feeling Good for Life* Aerobic Solution, you may be in the mood to try something new and more challenging. The

Feeling Good for Life Interval Training Solution is just the answer. The premise behind the *Feeling Good for Life* Interval Training Solution is simple: alternate short bursts of high-intensity exercise with periods of lower intensity. This type of training will not only get you in great cardiovascular shape, but also will also help you burn off fat faster then low-intensity aerobics.

How does the *Feeling Good for Life* Interval Training Solution burn more fat than low-intensity aerobics? It does this by dramatically speeding up your metabolism during and after your workout. First, during your *Feeling Good for Life* Interval Training Solution you will burn a greater amount of total calories than low-intensity aerobics. This means the more total calories you burn, the greater amount of fat you burn. But the *Feeling Good for Life* Interval Training Solution does not only burn more fat during your workout, but also causes you to burn a large amount of calories after you workout. In fact, a recent study conducted by Dr. J. King from East Tennessee State University found that fat burning after a workout was significantly greater in people who performed high intensity interval training. Their metabolic rate continued to stay elevated for a full 24 hours after their workout. What the *Feeling Good for Life* Interval Training Solution will do is allow you to continue burning more calories and fat throughout the whole day, helping you melt that bodyfat away.

One of the best things about the *Feeling Good for Life* Interval Training Solution is that it can be done with a number of activities. You can use it while running, cycling, on the stairclimber, or with any aerobic activity that you can alternate between periods of high and low intensity.

There are many different ways you can use the *Feeling Good for Life* Interval Training Solution. One that is great for outdoor activities, such as jogging, running, or sprinting up bleachers, is exercising at a low-to-moderate pace for 30–60 seconds and then going all out for 30–60 seconds. For this type of *Feeling Good for Life* Interval Training, start out at 4–6 minutes each session. You may be asking yourself, "Only 4–6 minutes?" But you will soon realize that going all out for 30–60 seconds for 4 or 5 intervals can be extremely intense and tiring.

Depending on your current level of cardiovascular fitness, you will have to experiment to find out how hard you can work during your *Feeling Good for Life* Interval Training Solution. You will do each interval workout 3 times per week (2 to 3 if you are also using the *Feeling Good for Life* Weight Training Solution). As you get more cardiovascularly fit, you are going to add 1–2 minutes each week until you reach 20 minutes. After this, it is not necessary to go beyond that, but rather focus on trying to work harder.

What if you are using the *Feeling Good for Life* Interval Training Solution indoors on a treadmill, stairclimber, or elliptical machine? You can use the same principles as I have described, but you will increase your intensity by changing the intensity levels of the machine. For example, you will start at level 2 on the stairclimber for the low-to-moderate 30–60 second period, then you will jack up the intensity to level 6 or 7 for 30–60 seconds and then back down to level 2 and repeat.

Another method you can use during your *Feeling Good for Life* Interval Training Solution is ascending interval training. Say you are on the elliptical machine and you are on level 3 for the first minute. For the second minute you are going increase the intensity to level 4. Then for the third minute you will go up to level 5 and for the fourth minute you will go up to level 6 and so on. After the fifth or sixth minute, you will drop back down to your starting level and then repeat the cycle for 20–25 minutes.

CHAPTER 3

The *Feeling Good for Life* Weight Training Solution

A Strong Body Will Build a Strong Mind

If you ever wanted to gain more muscle or lose a few pounds, weight training is one of the most effective ways to do it. Aerobic exercise will burn fat and get you cardiovascularly fit, but it will not help you build as much muscle as weight training. Weight training works by stressing your body, and forces your muscles to adapt by making them larger and stronger. However, weight training does not just help you tone-up and pack on the muscle, it also makes it easier for you to burn fat. Muscle is a very biologically active tissue that requires large amounts of energy in order to repair and maintain itself. Because your body has to expend more calories each day to build and keep that new muscle, weight training will automatically increase your metabolic rate. So even when you are just sitting around, simply having that extra muscle on your body will cause you to burn more calories and fat throughout the day.

Weight training not only helps you shape your body, but it also offers many other physical benefits such as improved cardiovascular function, lowered blood pressure, improved blood lipid levels, and decreased chances of developing diabetes. Weight training also protects your body against free radicals, metabolic by products that damage our cells and increase the risk of strokes, cancer, and other age-related disorders. Lifting weights is especially important for older people because it can give them greater mobility and ease the suffering of arthritis. Lastly, it increases bone density, which reduces the possibility of developing osteoporosis.

Weight Training Basics

Weight Training Equipment

You can use two types of equipment during your *Feeling Good for Life* Weight Training Solution: machines and/or free weights (e.g., barbells and dumbbells). I have included descriptions of 34 different machine and free weight exercise that you can choose from in appendix B. There are advantages and disadvantages for using both types of equipment, but most likely you will use a combination of the two for your *Feeling Good for Life* Weight Training Solution.

Weight Training Machines

One of the first things many people think when they see a weight training machine for the first time is that it looks so difficult to use. Although it may appear complicated at first, using the machine is relatively simple. Each machine has a seat and a bar that needs to be adjusted to your body size before you start using it. The machine is equipped with a bar attached to a weight stack that uses a pulley system to push or pull the weight. To use the machine, adjust the seat, bar height, and the amount of weight you will be using and then push or pull the weight accordingly.

Weight training machines are safe, versatile, and save time because you do not have to put on or remove any free weights from the bar. They keep you within a strict range of motion and show you the proper form necessary to thoroughly work the muscle. You also do not have to worry about balancing the weight, which can be a bit tricky for beginners. Machines are definitely good for those who are not experienced with weights and need to learn the proper form to work each muscle group.

Most machines display instructions on how to perform each of the exercises. When people are in the gym, many feel embarrassed to read these instructions because they think that other people will look at them and think they have no idea what they are doing. The truth is, when you go to the gym for the first time, you do not know exactly what you are trying to do and that is why the company has provided the instructions on the machine. More importantly, those same people that you think are looking at you didn't know how to use the equipment either when they first started.

There are also a number of home weight machines available that allow you to perform many different exercises for the entire body by using only one machine. These machines are good if you enjoy working out at home but they can be expensive ranging in price from $600 to $2000. If you decide to use one of these machines, read the instructions included with the machine on how to perform the exercise, but follow the *Feeling Good for Life* Weight Training Solutions in this chapter.

Free Weights

The two types of free weights you can use during you *Feeling Good for Life* Weight Training Solution are dumbbells and barbells. Dumbbells are the smaller weight bars you hold in each hand. They allow you to focus more on specific muscles. Barbells are long bars you hold with both hands and are used primarily in lifts involving many muscle groups at one time such as the bench press and squats.

Free weights allow you to perform a variety of exercises for each bodypart and allow you to work within your own natural range of motion. They will also increase coordination by strengthening the smaller muscle groups that help with balancing the weight. Learning to performing the movement properly takes some practice, so if this is your first time lifting weights, it might be better to start off with mostly machines and then move on to free weights.

Sets and Reps

A repetition (also called rep) refers to the number of times you lift the weight and a set refers to the number of repetitions you perform for that exercise. For example, if you lift the weight eight times (8 reps), that constitutes a set. The number of reps you do in a given set is determined by the amount of weight you use. You are going to have to experiment with the weight and find a resistance on each exercise that will allow you to perform the number of prescribed reps for each exercise.

Sequence of Exercises

Most exercises that work large muscle groups also involve the use of smaller muscle groups. Therefore, you should work the larger muscle groups, such as your chest and back before you work smaller ones, such as triceps and biceps. For example, in a bench press you not only use the larger chest muscles, but you also use the smaller shoulder and tricep muscles. In this movement, your chest is the strongest muscle and your triceps are the weakest. If you worked your triceps first, when you perform the bench press your triceps will tire out before the stronger chest muscles, resulting in your chest not getting as good of a workout. Working your muscles from largest to smallest allows you to do the most physically demanding exercises at the beginning of the workout when you are less fatigued, which makes for a more effective and safer workout.

Range of Motion

It is important that you perform each exercise through a complete range of motion. This means that you should lift the weight to the fully contracted position, lower it all the way back to the starting position, and then repeat. It will not benefit you to do partial reps for the sake of lifting more weight. One technique you can use to help perform the full range of motion is to lift the weight at a slow pace. Raising and lowering the weight in a slow, controlled manner requires a more even application of muscle force throughout the movement, which will make it easier for you to perform the exercise through the full range of motion.

Proper Breathing

When you are performing any weight training exercise, make a conscious effort not to hold your breath. When you hold your breath it can increase your blood pressure, resulting in a restriction of blood flow to the heart and coronary arteries. This can be avoided by simply inhaling when you lower the weight to the starting position, and exhaling when you lift the weight to the contracted position.

Warming Up and Cooling Down

You want to be sure to incorporate a good warm-up and cool-down as part of your *Feeling Good for Life* Weight Training Solution. The warm-up will prepare your body for the strenuous workout ahead and the cool-down will decrease muscle soreness and improve recovery time. Refer to chapter 2 for warm-up and cool-down guidelines.

Stretching It Out

Stretching is also an important component of the *Feeling Good for Life* Weight Training Solution. You can stretch before or after you workout, but my favorite time to stretch is in between sets. Stretching in between sets improves circulation and decreases the lactic acid and other metabolic waste that has built up in your muscle cells during your workout. It also saves time because you will not have to worry about stretching before or after you work out. Refer to chapter 2 for stretching guidelines.

What to Wear

There is nothing special that you have to wear when you train with weights. What you want is light, breathable clothing that you can move in. Loose fitting nylon or cotton gym shorts and a T-shirt should be fine. If you are using free weights, you may want to invest in a pair of weight lifting gloves so you don't get any blisters on your hands from squeezing and lifting the weights.

The 10-Week *Feeling Good for Life* Weight Training Solution

The 10-week *Feeling Good for Life* Weight Training Solution is divided into three phases. Phase #1 is meant to acquaint you with the gym and the new exercise you will be using. As you progress and gain confidence in your abilities you will gradually increase the exercise volume and intensity during Phase #2. Then in Phase #3, you are going to divide your body up in half so you can to add more exercises and focus on working individual muscle groups.

Phase #1: Weeks 1–2

During Phase #1 you will be training with weights 2 times a week, working your whole body each session. This is a time when you will start becoming familiar with the new movements and begin experimenting with the amount of weight you can use. Proper form is crucial to making sure you are thoroughly working the muscle. It is essential that you move the weight through the full range of motion. At first the exercises may seem a bit awkward, but after a couple of workouts your mind and body will have adapted and the movements will seem second nature.

Do not skip any bodypart during your 10-Week *Feeling Good for Life* Weight Training Solution. Many men tend to focus on working their upper body while women tend to work their lower body more. It is important that you exercise your entire body because if you only train a select few muscle groups, you are running the risk of developing a muscle imbalance and increasing your chances of injury.

Pick one exercise for each of the major body parts (quadriceps, ham-strings, chest, back, shoulders, biceps, triceps, abs, and calves) from appendix B. I have suggested which exercises you should start out with, but if you feel more comfortable performing a comparable exercise that is perfectly fine. If you are inexperienced with weight training, it is probably best to use machines for major muscle groups such as chest, back, and shoulders because they will force you to learn how to work these muscles properly. Remember to read the instructions in appendix B and set the machine properly for your body size.

You may be tempted to add more sets or use more weight, but I advise you not to do this. I want you to ease into your workouts and not do too much, too quickly. You need to give your body enough time to adjust to the new stress of weight training and get used to having this new activity in your life. More is not better. Focus on quality rather than quantity.

During the first 2 weeks you are going to perform 1–2 sets for 15 reps with the last rep being slightly hard to complete. When performing the exercises, you want to select a light enough resistance so that you can feel the muscle contract and relax as you take it through the correct range of motion. If you can complete 15 reps with little effort, you may have to use a heavier weight. If you can't do 15 reps, then the weight is too heavy so decrease the weight on your next set or workout. Rest anywhere between 30–60 seconds in between each exercise.

Phase #2: Weeks 3–4

After 2 weeks you are still going to do 2 workout sessions per week, but now you are going to increase the number of sets to 3. During your work-outs, the weight you will be using should be harder then the last 2 weeks, but not so heavy that you cannot complete 12 full reps. When you are able to lift the weight more than 12 times with ease, it means that you have gotten stronger and need more resistance so you can perform 12 hard reps. Increase the weight by about 5–10 percent of the weight you are currently using. After you finish a set, rest 1–2 minutes to allow your body enough time to recover before you begin the next set or exercise.

Muscle Group	Exercise	Phase #1 (Weeks 1–2)		Phase #2 (Weeks 3–4)	
		Sets	Reps	Sets	Reps
Quads/Glutes	Leg Press	1–2	15	3	12
Hamstrings	Leg Curl	1–2	15	3	12
Back	Pulldown	1–2	15	3	12
Chest	Machine Chest Press	1–2	15	3	12
Shoulders	Machine Shoulder Press	1–2	15	3	12
Trapezius	Dumbbell Shrug	1–2	15	3	12
Triceps	Pushdown	1–2	15	3	12
Biceps	Seated Bicep Curl	1–2	15	3	12
Calves	Standing Calf Raise	1–2	15	3	12
Abs	Crunch	1–2	15	3	12
Lower Back	Back Extension	1–2	15	3	12

Phase #3: Weeks 5–10

Now that you have become familiar with the exercises and working your muscles using the proper range of motion, it is time to try something new to keep your body adapting. You are now going to divide your body up into two parts (upper body for day 1 and lower body for day 2) and train 3 days a week on non-consecutive days (i.e., Monday, Wednesday, Friday). The reason we divide up your body in this manner is so you can perform more exercises each session to increase your focus on each muscle group. You should allow at least 2 days of rest in between workout sessions. If you miss a workout, don't try to double up and work out 2 days in a row. Simply shift your workout schedule one day and pick up where you left off. It is all right if you miss a day every so often, just don't make it a habit.

In Phase #3 you also have the option to add variety to your workouts by starting to use more barbell and dumbbell exercises. Refer to appendix B to make sure you are performing the new free weight exercises properly. It is essential that you do not use a weight so heavy that it hinders your form. Remember that the restricted range of motion of a machine no longer balances the weight, so it is necessary to perform the free weight movements in a slow, controlled manner.

Phase #3

Workout #1: Upper Body

Muscle Group	Exercise	Sets	Reps
Chest	Flat Bench Fly	3	10-12
	Incline Press	3	10-12
Back	Pulldown	3	10-12
	One Arm- Dumbbell Row	3	10-12
Shoulders	Seated Dumbbell Press	3	10-12
	Side Lateral Raise	2	10-12
Traps	Dumbbell Shrug	3	10-12
Triceps	Pushdown	3	10-12
	Triceps Kickback	2	10-12
Bicep	Incline Curl	3	10-12
	Concentration Curl	2	10-12

Workout #2: Lower Body

Muscle Group	Exercise	Sets	Reps
Quads/Glutes	Leg Extension	3	10-12
	Leg Press	3	10-12
Hamstring	Leg Curl	3	10-12
Calves	Standing Calf Raise	3	10-12
Lower back	Back Extension	3	12-15
Abs	Crunch	3	12-15
	Knee Raise	2	12-15

The 10-Week *Feeling Good for Life* Weight Training Solution

Week	Monday	Tuesday	Wednesday	Thursday	Friday	Sat/Sun
1		Whole Body 1 Set 15 Reps		Whole Body 1 Set 15 Reps		
2		Whole Body 1 Set 15 Reps		Whole Body 1 Set 15 Reps		
3		Whole Body 2 Sets 12 Reps		Whole Body 2 Sets 12 Reps		
4		Whole Body 2 Sets 12 Reps		Whole Body 2 Sets 12 Reps		
5	Workout #1 Upper Body		Workout #2 Lower Body		Workout #1 Upper Body	
6	Workout #2 Lower Body		Workout #1 Upper Body		Workout #2 Lower Body	
7	Workout #1 Upper Body		Workout #2 Lower Body		Workout #1 Upper Body	
8	Workout #2 Lower Body		Workout #1 Upper Body		Workout #2 Lower Body	
9	Workout #1 Upper Body		Workout #2 Lower Body		Workout #1 Upper Body	
10	Workout #2 Lower Body		Workout #1 Upper Body		Workout #2 Lower Body	

Advanced *Feeling Good for Life* Weight Training Solutions

After using the 10-week *Feeling Good for Life* Weight Training Solution, you may want to try something new and focus on specific goals you may have such as improving muscular endurance, accelerating fat loss, or building more muscle. I have included 3 Advanced *Feeling Good for Life* Weight Training Solutions to help you accomplish these goals.

The *Feeling Good for Life* Muscular Endurance Solution

Many of you enjoy activities such as basketball, tennis, or other sports that require powerful movements for a prolonged period of time. By using the *Feeling Good for Life* Muscular Endurance Solution, you will become quicker, more agile, and increase your stamina. The key element in this type of training is for you to keep your body constantly moving during your workout. This is accomplished by doing a circuit workout–performing one exercise right after another, eliminating as much rest as possible in between exercises. Performing your workout without pausing will exercise your body anaerobiclly through weight training and aerobically by moving continuously and keeping your heart rate up.

During the *Feeling Good for Life* Muscular Endurance Solution you will use the same upper body/lower body split as Phase #3 of the *Feeling Good for Life* 10-week Weight Training Solution. Pick one exercise for each bodypart and perform 3 circuits during each workout. After you have completed one circuit, rest for a couple of minutes and then repeat the circuit a second and third time. Use a weight that will allow you to perform 12–15 reps. To add variety to your workouts, you can switch up any of the exercise in appendix B, just make sure that you are always performing one exercise for each major muscle group. As you continue to get into better shape, you can increase the number of circuits to 4–5.

The *Feeling Good for Life* Fat Loss Solution

Most people who want to decrease their bodyfat turn to aerobic exercise machines such as the treadmill and stairclimber first because these forms of exercise are associated with burning the most fat. It is true that aerobic exercise burns more fat calories during a workout, but one downside to aerobic exercise is that your metabolism can slow back down to normal levels within about half an hour after your workout (if the exercise is not very intense). This is certainly not the case for weight training.

After you lift weights, your metabolic rate will stay elevated for many hours, resulting in more calories burned. Also, chapter 2 explained how muscle is a very active tissue and your body requires more energy to maintain a pound of muscle than a pound of fat. Therefore, increasing your muscle through weight training automatically increase your metabolic rate. So if fat loss is your goal, combining weight training with aerobic exercise will ignite your internal furnace and cause you to burn bodyfat faster than doing either one alone.

If you just finished the 10-week *Feeling Good for Life* Weight Training Solution, start out by adding 20 minutes of the *Feeling Good for Life* Aerobic Solution 2 times a week. You can either do this on separate days or do it after your weight training session. You can use any of the *Feeling Good for Life* Aerobic Solution exercises described in chapter 2. Then every week add 3–5 minutes to each session until you get to 35 minutes. When you get to this point, it is not necessary to continue to increase the duration of your workouts. What you should focus on is how hard you are working and try to increase the intensity of each workout. For example, if you are doing 30 minutes at 4.5 miles per hour on the treadmill, each week try to increase the intensity by .1 or .2. You will burn a greater amount of calories and fat and will keep your metabolism elevated longer from high intensity/short duration workouts than long workouts at a mild to moderate pace. After a month, add 1 more aerobic workout but do not do more than 3 aerobic works per week because doing too much aerobic work will hinder muscle growth. If you have completed the 10-week *Feeling Good for Life* Aerobic Solution, begin the 10-week *Feeling Good for Life* Weight Training Solution and lower your aerobic work to 20–30 minutes, 2–3 times per week.

Notice that I have been using the phrase "fat loss" rather then "weight loss." I do this to stress that you should be focusing on losing bodyfat and not simply on losing weight. There are hundreds of quick loss diets or radical exercise routines and many of them actually do cause you to lose weight, but not the weight you want to lose. For example, many of you have probably heard of the low-carbohydrate diet that forces your body to lose weight. It is true that you will lose a significant amount of weight on this type of diet, but not much of it is from fat. Most of the weight you will lose will be from water because for every gram of carbohydrate you store, there are three grams of water attached to it. So when you drop your carbohydrates, you are actually forcing your body to excrete water and this accounts for most of the weight you lose on a low-carbohydrate diet. Worst of all, once you begin eating carbohydrates again most of the weight you lost will come back because your body will try to reabsorb all the water.

Another method people use to try to lose weight is to exercise hard and often. These people soon find themselves tired and have little fat loss to show for all their hard work. This is because exercising too much can throw you into a state of overtraining, resulting in the breakdown of muscle for energy to sustain the excessive exercising. Muscle is the last thing you want to lose because when you decrease your muscle mass, it slows down your metabolic rate and makes losing bodyfat an uphill battle. It is physiologically impossible (unless you use illegal drugs) to lose a large amount of weight in a healthy manner in a short period of time. Physiologically our bodies don't work like that. Healthy weight loss ranges between 1 to 2 pounds of fat per week.

A few last tips before we move on. First, don't use the scale to measure your progress. Your weight can fluctuate 2–5 pounds throughout the day depending on what you eat and drink. One day the scale says you lost 3 pounds and the next day it says you lost 2 pounds. The best thing to do is weigh yourself first thing in the morning and then put the scale away for a few months.

One great way to measure your progress is to get your bodyfat measured, either at a local gym or you can get some skin calipers and measure your bodyfat on your own. By using this valuable tool, you will measure your progress more accurately and make sure you are losing fat and not muscle or water. You can also measure your progress by clothing size or by measuring your body size. You can use a measuring tape around your chest, arms, waist and thigh and check the measurement every month to see if you are on track.

A quick note about eating before you work out. You should not eat a large amount of carbohydrates before or during your workout if you goal is to lose bodyfat. I will discuss this in greater detail in the *Nutrition-4-Life* chapter, but for now I want you to keep in mind that if you eat something with lots of carbohydrates before your workout, especially sugars, it will prevent you from burning fat during your workout. Carbohydrates will raise your insulin levels, which will inhibit the enzyme that is used to breakdown fat. It is best to eat about 2 hours or so before you workout. If you feel that you need to eat something close to your workout, eat something very light such as a nutritional bar or an apple. Just make sure that is contains a low to moderate amount of carbohydrates.

Keep in mind that the *Feeling Good for Life* Fat Loss Solution is a greater commitment than the other *Feeling Good for Life* Solutions because you will have to exercise a few more times per week or train for a longer period of time. It can be a bit difficult to go to the gym or workout at home 4–5 days a week or work out for up to an hour and a half each session, so start out gradually and then work your way up to a level and frequency of exercise that fits into your life.

The *Feeling Good for Life* Muscle Building Solution

If your goal is to build muscle and increase strength, then this is the program for you. In the *Feeling Good for Life* Muscle Building Solution you are going to split up your body into three separate workouts so you can use more exercises for each muscle group. This will allow you to work the muscle with a greater intensity to stimulate the most muscle growth from your workouts.

The main principle of *Feeling Good for Life* Muscle Building Solution is to consistently put your muscles under a form of stress they are not accustomed to and force them to adapt by making your muscles larger and stronger. We can accomplish this through progressively overloading the muscle by either doing more sets or increasing the intensity of the workouts. Since you don't want to stay in the gym for hours, it is more efficient and effective to increase the intensity of the workout sessions rather than increase the number of sets.

When thinking about muscle growth, it helps to keep this analogy in mind. Say you take a piece of sandpaper and start rubbing it against your palm. You will soon break the skin and form a cut. When you take away the sandpaper and let your hand recover for a few days, the cut will heal. After your skin repairs itself to its previous state, a magical thing happens—your body overcompensates this healing process by forming a callus and making that area stronger. It does this so the next time it encounters the same type of stress, your body will be prepared and the sandpaper won't cause as much damage. Well, this exact same process happens when you work out with weights.

When you work your muscles through weight training, you are actually making micro-tears in your muscles, causing damage to your muscle cells. After an intense weight training workout, your muscles go through the same healing process and not until you recover back to your original state does the overcompensation phase of making your muscles bigger and stronger take place. Your body adapts so that the next time you lift the same amount of weight, your muscles will be prepared and won't receive as much damage. This is why it is necessary to progressively overload your muscles with more weight. If you use the same weight over and over again, you would not be putting enough stress on your body to force them to adapt and grow.

Now think of this: What if you continued to rub the sandpaper again and again while your palm was trying to heal itself? If you did this, then your body would never complete the recovery phase and enter the overcompensation phase to form a callus. Well, if you exercise too often you will be inhibiting your body from adapting and growing. Your muscles are not going to get bigger and stronger if you do not allow them enough time to rest so if you keep exercising without allowing yourself to completely recover, you will stay in the healing phase and never reach the overcompensation or "growth" phase. It is only when you allow your body to completely finish healing itself that you will start to see an increase in muscle growth and strength.

To stimulate the most muscle growth from your workouts, you will need to train at a higher intensity then what you have previously been doing. Performing sets at a higher intensity is an extremely important factor in stimulating muscle growth. Let's use your bicep muscles to explain this principle.

Your bicep muscles (as well as every other muscle in your body) are made up of hundreds to thousands of muscle fibers that contract individually to perform work. To make things simple, let's say that you have 2,000 total muscle fibers in both of your bicep muscles. You are working your biceps today with barbell curls and for your first set, you will use 40 pounds to try to get 8–10 reps. For the first rep, your biceps use 500 fibers to lift the weight. For the second rep, your biceps use those same 500 fibers, but since they are a bit fatigued from the last rep your body will recruit 150 more fibers to complete the second rep. On the third rep, those 650 fibers bring up the weight, but they too are fatigued from the second rep, so another 150 are recruited to bring up the weight. This recruitment process continues until you have used and tired out all your available muscle fibers and have reached muscular failure—the point at which you can no longer lift the weight up. At this point nearly all your bicep muscle fibers have been utilized during the exercise; therefore, when you recruit as many muscle fibers as you can during a set, you are stimulating the most muscle growth. This is why the last rep is so important in achieving the most muscle growth and is what you should be aiming for during your workout sessions.

Each exercise you perform should be done so in the following manner. The first set should be relatively light, allowing you to perform 12–15 reps fairly easy. This first set is meant to warm-up your muscles by getting blood flowing to the specific areas that you are about to work. For the second set you are going to increase the weight to provide the muscle with more resistance and do 10–12 reps. After the second set you will be prepared to do your last "main" set. On this last set you are going to go to failure (do as many reps as you can) with a weight that will land you in the 8–10 rep range for upper body and 10–12 for lower body. Going to failure will stimulate the most fibers for the greatest muscle growth.

To get used to this type of training, only do 1 set to failure for the first month. Your body as well as your mental state are not used to such high intensity training, so allow enough time to adjust to your workouts. After 4–6 weeks, you can add 1 more set to failure for each exercise. After adding this set, it is not necessary to do more sets to failure. Continuing to increase the number of sets will not result in a significant increase in muscle stimulation and will only deplete the limited energy resources you have for recovery and building muscle. Remember, do not ascribe the economical principle of "more is better" or you will soon enter an overtraining state, which will only lead to fatigue and decreased muscle growth.

Because you will be training with greater intensity, it is going to take longer for your muscles to recover from each workout. Therefore, you are going to allow each bodypart to rest for 5 or 6 days. In the *Feeling Good for Life* Muscle Building Solution you are going to divide your body into three different days. You can split this up anyway you want. For example, you can work out every other day so each bodypart gets 6 days of rest or you can double up two of the workouts so each bodypart is worked every 5 days. You can decide which split works best for you depending on how much time you have available to you.

The *Feeling Good for Life* Muscle Building Solution

Workout # 1

Muscle Group	Exercise	Sets	Reps
Chest	1) Flat Bench Fly	1	12-15
	2) Incline Press	1	10-12
	3) Bench Press	1	8-10
Back	1) Pulldown	1	12-15
	2) One-Arm Dumbbell Row	1	10-12
	3) Back Extension	1	8-10
Bicep	1) Barbell Curl	1	12-15
	2) Incline Curl	1	10-12
	3) Concentration Curl	1	8-10
Triceps	1) Pushdown	1	12-15
	2) Overhead Extension	1	10-12
	3) Lying Tricep Extension	1	8-10

Workout #2

Muscle Group	Exercise	Sets	Reps
Quads/Glutes	1) Leg Extension	1	15
	2) Leg Press/Squat	1	12-15
	3) Lunge	1	10-12
Hamstring	1) Seated Leg Curl	1	15
		1	12-15
		1	10-12
Shoulders	1) Seated Dumbbell Press	1	12-15
	2) Side Lateral Raise	1	10-12
	3) Front Raise	1	8-10
Calves	1) Standing Calf Raise	1	15
	2) Seated Calf Raise	1	12-15
		1	10-12
Abs	1) Incline Crunch	1	15
	2) Knee Raise	1	12-15
		1	10-12

The *Feeling Good for Life* Home Workout

Many people may not want to use a gym for their *Feeling Good for Life* Muscle Building Solution and this is why I have included recommendations for a *Feeling Good for Life* Home Workout. Training at home can be very convenient. There is no need to commute, it is time-efficient because there is no wait to use the equipment, and most importantly, you can do it in the privacy of your own home. The main thing I want is for you to find a place where you feel comfortable using your *Feeling Good for Life* Weight Training Solution.

A home gym can be inexpensive and not very difficult to set up. All you need is a set of adjustable dumbbells and an adjustable weight bench. The dumbbells should allow you to change the amount of weight depending on the exercises you are performing. Men should get dumbbells that can adjust to at least 50 pounds and women to at least 25 pounds. The bench should allow you to do flat as well as incline movements at varying degrees. Find a place in your house that is well lit, well ventilated, and if possible, has a full-length mirror so you can check to see if you are doing the exercises properly. You may also want to have a CD player or radio to play music that will motivate you.

The *Feeling Good for Life* Home Workout is the same routine as the 10-Week *Feeling Good for Life* Weight Training Solution with the exception of a few different exercises. Simply look at the dumbbell exercise in appendix B and substitute the appropriate exercise for each muscle group.

Chapter 4

Nutrition-4-Life™

Fuel Your Body, Fuel Your Mind

Think about what's involved in building a house. One of the main things you have to do is find the proper tools and materials needed to build the kind of house you want. You certainly don't want to use just anything you can find and put them together willy-nilly and call it your house. Certain materials have specific functions and you need to know what each piece of material is used for. You also need to know how and when to put each piece in its proper place and this requires you have a detailed plan, a blueprint that shows you exactly what you need to do to create the structure of your dreams.

Well, this same approach applies to developing the proper diet needed for you to begin *Feeling Good for Life*. However, instead of using wood, metal, glass, and plastic, you are going to use specific foods and special supplements to create a dietary roadmap that will help you achieve all your mental and physical health goals. *Nutriton-4-Life* is a specially formulated nutritional system consisting of 4 unique elements that work synergistically to help you burn fat, build muscle, and elevate your mood.

The first element of *Nutriton-4-Life* is the *40-40-20 Solution,* which is a precise ratio of protein, carbohydrates, and fat that will enhance your body's natural medicines and provide you with the nutrients needed to put you in a mental and physical anabolic state that is ideal for melting away bodyfat, increasing muscle, and boosting your mood. You will see that the *40-40-20 Solution* is one of the easiest methods you can use to figure out how much you should be eating and in what proportions. The second element of *Nutriton-4-Life* is 8 specialized dietary techniques that will boost the nutritional powers of the *40-40-20 Solution* and make it easy to incorporate healthy eating into your life. The third element involves the use of the latest scientifically tested supplements, such as omega-3 fatty acids and alpha lipoic acid which have the ability to dramatically improve your mood, decrease your risk of numerous chronic illnesses, stabilize insulin and blood sugar levels, and help you lose fat and tone up. The final component of *Nutrition-4-Life* is, of course, the *Feeling Good for Life* Exercise Solution. This combination of the *40-40-20 Solution,* specialized dietary techniques, super supplements, and the *Feeling Good for Life* Exercise Solution makes up *Nutriton-4-Life* and will work synergistically to help you get in the best shape of your life both mentally and physically.

The *40-40-20*™ *Solution*

TAt the heart of *Nutrion-4-Life* is the *40-40-20 Solution,* which is a special ratio of 40% protein, 40% carbohydrates, and 20% fat. The *40-40-20 Solution* differs from other diets that prescribe a certain macronutrient intake in that the *40-40-20 Solution* emphasizes not only the value of eating a specific ratio of protein, carbohydrates, and fat, but also the importance of what type of macronutrients you eat. There are numerous types of protein, carbohydrates, and fats out there, so it is crucial that you take in the "good" sources of these nutrients. This precise ratio of 40% protein, 40% carbohydrates, and 20% fat will balance out your body's chemistry, unlock your fat-burning, muscle-building potential, and will allow your body to release its natural medicines, such as serotonin and endorphins to help you begin *Feeling Good for Life.*

Protein Power

Protein can be thought of as the "creating" nutrient because it provides the basic materials needed to create and repair the tissues in your body. When you ingest protein, it is broken down into molecules called amino acids that serve as the building blocks for a multitude of bodily processes, such as the creation of hormones, enzymes, and other molecules needed for metabolism and proper bodily functioning.

Your body is constantly in a balancing act in which it is continually breaking down and rebuilding itself. If you are exercising regularly and not giving your body a consistent supply of protein and amino acids, you will negatively alter this breakdown/rebuilding balance and begin tearing down existing protein (i.e., hard-earned muscle) in order for your body to repair itself. This is the last thing you want happening because when your body breaks down its own protein for energy, it forces your metabolism to slow down, making it harder for you to build muscle and burn fat. This is why it is absolutely necessary that you get enough protein throughout the day. Your goal should be to consume enough protein to positively tip the balance of this breakdown/rebuilding process by providing your body with the protein needed to put you into a mental and physical anabolic state.

Researchers have demonstrated that people who exercise regularly, especially those who lift weights, need more protein than the average person. It has also been known for some time now that when you combine weight training with additional protein, you gain more muscle. And as you read in chapter 3, the more muscle you gain, the higher your metabolic rate and fat-burning potential. Protein itself also has thermogenic properties to it, meaning it takes significantly more energy to break down protein than carbohydrates or fat, so you will actually be burning more calories just by eating additional protein.

So how much protein should you eat? You are going to consume at least 1 gram of protein for every pound of bodyweight. So if you are a man who weighs 180 pounds, you are going to eat at least 1 gram of protein per pound of bodyweight and if you are a woman who weighs 120 pounds, you are going to eat 120 grams of protein. Sounds easy enough? Well it is, and the *40-40-20 Solution* will not make you do any long calculations and calorie counting like all the other diets out there. It is just two simple steps: find out your weight and eat the same amount of protein in grams.

Eating quality protein is just as important as eating the right amount of protein. It is crucial that you eat quality proteins high in essential amino acids (those that cannot be synthesized by our bodies) because when your body is deficient, it can hinder muscle growth and improvement in your mood. At the end of the *40-40-20 Solution* section I have provided a list of *40-40-20 Solution* Power Foods where you will find great sources of proteins that have large quantities of essential amino acids.

Are High Protein Diets Bad for You?

You may have read in magazines and other nutrition books that high-protein diets are bad for you and can cause many negative side effects. Although the *40-40-20 Solution* uses a higher amount of protein than other diets, I want you to realize that the *40-40-20 Solution* is not a high-protein diet in the traditional sense. What many doctors and researchers are negatively referring to is the high protein/low carbohydrate diets that have recently become popular again. Critics of these diets are correct in their condemnation. By going on one of these high protein/low carbohydrate diets for a prolonged period of time, you can experience many negative side effects, such as low blood sugar levels, insulin imbalances, mood swings, and provide too little fuel for the brain to function properly.

It is true that you can lose weight on a diet like this, but much of that weight loss comes from water and muscle, which is going to slow down your metabolism and make burning fat an uphill battle. These diets are also hard to follow because they forbid you from consuming foods that you really like to eat and naturally crave. What *Nutrition-4-Life* teaches you is that balance and portion control are the keys to formulating a proper diet. The ratio of 40% protein, 40% carbohydrates, and 20% fat of the *40-40-20 Solution* will eliminate the negative side effects you can experience on high protein/low carbohydrate diets.

Carbohydrate Control

The recent trend in low-carbohydrate diets has given carbohydrates a bad rap. The truth is that carbohydrates are good for us and are an essential part of our diet. They are the main energy source during exercise and are necessary for proper brain function. If you don't eat enough carbohydrates, you are headed down a dark path with many negative side effects that will put a halt to your mental and physical health goals.

It is the *excessive* amount of carbohydrates we eat that are bad for us. Just like you should not ascribe to the economic principle of "more is better" during your *Feeling Good for Life* Exercise Solution, you should not do it during *Nutrition-4-Life*, especially when it comes to eating carbohydrates. Consuming too many carbohydrates can make you sleepy, sluggish, moody, and pack on those unwanted pounds of fat. Worst of all, when you eat a lot of carbohydrates, you will raise your insulin levels and prevent your body from burning bodyfat. So if you eat a bagel or something with lots of carbohydrates before you do aerobic work, you will be blocking your body from breaking down fat for energy.

However, if you eat the right type of carbohydrates, in specific amounts, at precise times, you will optimize your body's ability to burn fat, build muscle, and boost your mood. You must always keep in mind that you have the power to control how your body reacts to food. In this part of the *40-40-20 Solution,* I will teach you how to control your bodily reaction to carbohydrates by eating the proper foods in the correct portions, with the right amount of protein and fat.

A Carbohydrate is Not a Carbohydrate

All carbohydrates are not created equal. Different carbohydrates have different effects on your body's chemistry and learning which carbohydrates will bring you down or put you in a physical and mental anabolic state is one of the keys to begin *Feeling Good for Life*.

Carbohydrates can be divided up into two categories: simple sugars and complex carbohydrates. Examples of simple sugars are glucose, fructose, and refined sugars, such as sucrose. Sources of complex carbohydrates are potatoes, pasta, breads, and beans. The simpler the carbohydrate, the quicker it gets broken down into sugar and released into your bloodstream and the more complex the carbohydrate, the longer it takes to be broken down and carried to your cells to be burned for energy.

When carbohydrates enter our digestive system, our body tries to stabilize blood sugar levels through the use of the hormone insulin. Certain carbohydrates will increase insulin activity in the blood more than others. Simple carbohydrates are rapidly converted into sugars and quickly enter the blood to trigger a large insulin response whereas complex carbohydrates are broken down slowly and gradually enter the bloodstream resulting in a mild and progressively elevated blood sugar and insulin response. What you are going to focus on in the *40-40-20 Solution* is to avoid eating simple sugars as much as possible.

You see, whenever you eat that snack full of simple sugars, you are going to cause insulin to rise rapidly and quickly transport sugar out of the blood and into your muscle cells and liver. This large spike in insulin will cause your blood sugar levels to plummet, sending a hunger signal to your brain that you need more food to restore your blood sugar levels back to normal. When you have low blood sugar levels, you can experience a number of negative symptoms, such as dizziness, lack of concentration, and moodiness. When you eventually decide to satisfy that hunger signal caused by insulin's hyperactivity, you will most likely grab another sweet snack high in simple sugars and the process of spiked insulin levels and low blood sugar will start all over again, turning into a vicious cycle. However, the worst part is that your liver and muscles can only store a limited amount of carbohydrates, so when insulin and sugar levels are too high, it turns on the enzyme in fat cells called lipoprotein lipase, which causes your body to store the excess sugar in the worst possible place: your fat cells.

This is why it is necessary to try to eat more complex carbohydrates and limit simple sugars. Complex carbohydrates will not spike insulin levels (unless you eat a large quantity, but the *40-40-20 Solution* will prevent you from doing this). In the list of *40-40-20 Solution* Power Foods, I have included the best sources of complex carbohydrates that will help stabilize your blood sugar levels and give your body a steady supply of energy throughout the day.

However, eating the right type of carbohydrates is only part of the solution to controlling your insulin levels. You also have the power to control the way your body reacts to carbohydrates by controlling how many carbohydrates you eat as well as by manipulating your protein/carbohydrate/fat ratio. Using the *40-40-20 Solution* ratio of 40% protein, 40% carbohydrates, and 20% fat will act as the glue that will hold your *Nutrition-4-Life* Diet together and put your mind and body into a prime *Feeling Good for Life* state. Following the strict ratio of the *40-40-20 Solution* will also help you regulate how many carbohydrates you eat, which will enhance insulin stabilization and eliminate the chances of those carbohydrates turning into fat.

Stabilizing Insulin with the *40-40-20 Solution*

The next step in controlling how your body reacts to carbohydrates is the manipulation of another hormone responsible for the regulation of blood sugar and insulin levels. This powerful hormone is glucogon and it plays a critical role in whether or not you are in an anabolic mental and physical state.

You can think of insulin and glucogon as biological opposites where insulin is primarily a "storage" hormone and glucogon is a "metabolizing" hormone. Insulin's main job is to remove glucose (sugars) from the blood stream and convert glucose into glycogen and store it into your liver, muscle, or fat cells. Glucogon's primary responsibility is the release of glycogen in the form of glucose and maintaining tight control over blood sugar levels though the inhibition of insulin activity. The balance of these two hormones is crucial to unlocking your *Feeling Good for Life* potential and is dependent on two factors: how much you eat, specifically carbohydrates (because excess calories will cause an increase in insulin and inhibit glucogon) and the protein/carbohydrate/fat makeup of the foods you consume.

You know that simple sugars will increase your insulin levels, but also eating too many carbohydrates, whether they are simple or complex, will also spike insulin activity. That big bowl of pasta or couple of large baked potatoes can swell your insulin levels, so it is also necessary to regulate the amount of carbohydrates you eat. How do you find out what this amount is? The *40-40-20 Solution* makes this answer very easy.

Since you have already found out how much protein you need to eat using your body weight, all you have to do is eat the same amount of carbohydrates as you do protein. Yes, it's that simple! So if you are a man who weighs 180 pounds, you will eat at least 180 grams of protein and 180 grams of carbohydrates. If you are a woman who weighs 130, then will eat 130 grams of both protein and carbohydrates. That is the beauty of the *40-40-20 Solution*: find your bodyweight and then eat the same amount of protein and carbohydrates in grams. Every meal you eat (except your last meal which I will explain in the *40-40-20 Solution* Exception) should have an equal amount of protein and carbohydrates in it.

So why do you eat the same amount of protein and carbohydrates at each meal? Why can't you eat one meal of only carbohydrates and then have a protein meal later in the day that consists of the same amount of carbohydrates you ate? We already talked about the vicious insulin cycle that happens when you eat only carbohydrates, so you know you shouldn't eat this type of meal. Now if you only eat pure protein, chances are that a large percentage of this protein will be converted into blood sugar and burned for energy. This is why it is vital that you follow the *40-40-20 Solution* and mix and match your carbohydrates and protein. First, eating an adequate amount of protein stimulates glucogon, which will blunt insulin activity caused by carbohydrates and stabilize insulin levels. Glucogon also mobilizes the breakdown of stored bodyfat and helps transport it directly into your blood stream, allowing your muscles to use the fat for energy instead of carbohydrates. Second, carbohydrates have a protein "sparing" effect which means that by combing an equal amount of carbohydrates and protein, your body will preferentially use more carbohydrates and fat for fuel and spare your valuable protein for the creation of critical enzymes, hormones, and muscle. Lastly, when you eat protein and carbohydrates in the same meal, it increases nutrient absorption allowing your body to utilize protein and carbohydrates more efficiently than eating either one alone.

The *40-40-20 Solution* Exception

There is one meal of the day that you are not going to follow the *40-40-20 Solution* and that is the last meal of the day, specifically right before you go to bed. Instead of eating an equal amount of protein and carbohydrates at this time, you are going to eat a meal of pure protein. This is because during sleep, your body enters a state of rest and recuperation where your body repairs your muscles, rejuvenates major hormones, and restores vital neurochemicals in your brain. To do this, your body needs a supply of quality nutrients to use during this recovery phase. By eating a meal of pure protein, you can tap into and accelerate this recuperation period by supplying the proper materials needed for muscle growth, hormone production, and brain repair.

So why not eat carbohydrates along with the protein? During sleep your metabolism dramatically slows down and eating carbohydrates at this time increases the chance these carbohydrates will be stored as fat. It also takes more energy to break down protein therefore, there is little chance that any of it will turn into fat.

It is best to use a protein that will be absorbed slowly by the body. This can be low fat turkey, chicken, or my favorite, non-fat cottage cheese. Non-fat cottage cheese is probably the best food you can eat at this time because it is made out of to special proteins called whey and casein. Whey protein gets absorbed fairly quickly giving your body a quick supply of protein while casein has unique properties to it, which allow it to be digested very slowly in your stomach. This allows your body to have a constant supply of protein for a prolonged period of time and provides the necessary nutrients needed for your body to repair and heal itself through-out the night.

Fat is not a Four-Letter-Word

"Cut back on your fat," is a phrase that has been resonating throughout America for the past 15 years. There is some merit to this saying. Too much fat will put you at risk for many health problems and will also make you fat. As a result, many people are fat-phobic and try to avoid fat at all costs. But the truth is that all fats are not bad. There are both good and bad fats and consuming too many bad fats is the main cause of chronic illness and widespread obesity seen in America today.

So when someone tells you to eliminate all the fat from your diet, you are being misinformed. Fat performs many vital functions. It is necessary for the construction of our cell membranes; it is a shock absorber for vital organs; it's an insulator for the nervous system; it is essential for healthy hair, nails and skin; and is a major source of energy during exercise. Also, when you eat fat in a meal, it slows down the digestion and absorption of carbohydrates, so glucose trickles gradually into the blood, providing a steady supply of glucose to your muscle cells. So don't cut out all the fat from your diet. What you need to focus on is eating the right type of fat. Saturated fats such as butter, margarine, and most fried foods are the bad fats and should be avoided at all costs. Unsaturated fats, such as canola oil, olive oil, sesame oil, evening promise oil, and the fat in avocados are the ones that are good for you.

How much fat should you be eating? There is going to be fat in the protein and carbohydrates you eat, so if you eat relatively clean foods you should be getting the 20% needed for the *40-40-20 Solution*. It is not necessary to count the grams of fat you are eating each day, so long as you stick to eating the *40-40-20 Solution* Power Foods I have listed. Don't get bogged down in counting calories. The main focus of the 20% fat component of the *40-40-20 Solution* is the type of fat you are eating rather than how much. Actually, you can eat even less than 20% fat in your diet so long as you consume enough of the fats I will discuss in the Essential Fatty Acid (EFA) and Omega-3 Solution in this chapter. This section will show you how to change your food intake and supplement your diet with certain fatty acids so you can get the proper amount and right type of fats needed for you to begin *Feeling God for Life*.

Vegetables

Vegetables are one of the best foods that you can eat during your *40-40-20 Solution*. These foods are high in vitamins and minerals and a great source of fiber. Vegetables help manage insulin levels by slowing down absorption, are low in calories and contain valuable antioxidants. You can eat as many vegetables as you want, just make sure to get at least 2–3 servings each day.

Bringing It All Together—The Big 8

#1–Eat 5–6 *40-40-20 Solution* Meals a Day

Consuming three square meals a day is no longer the way to get in shape both mentally and physically. You must eat to burn fat, build muscle, and elevate your mood. I know that this may sound counterintuitive, especially in trying to lose bodyfat, but depriving yourself of much-needed nutrients will spoil your chances to begin *Feeling Good for Life*. In fact, not eating enough will actually slow down your metabolism, increase your chances of storing bodyfat, and depress your mood.

Many people think that reducing their calories will force their body to burn lots of fat, but in reality, it does the exact opposite. You see, our bodies have not changed very much biologically over the past 100,000 years and still consider themselves in a survival mode. When you dramatically reduce you caloric intake or eat only a couple of times per day, your body sends itself into a state of alarm, thinking it is beginning to starve. The calories it needs are no longer available, so it takes preventative measures to conserve its energy.

At first your body will shift its energy sources and begin using more fat for fuel, but this is short-lived and your body will soon start burning protein, specifically your hard-earned muscle. Next, one of the major ways your body will begin trying to conserve energy is through a reduction in body heat. In order for your body to stay at the optimal temperature of 98.5 degrees, your body has to burn a large quantity of calories each day. What your body will do when it is not getting enough calories is drop your body temperature, which is going to slow down your metabolism and decrease the amount of calories you burn throughout the day. However, there is an even more disastrous measure your body takes to conserve energy. What do you think the best insulator of body heat is? You guessed it—fat. Dropping your calories results in your body becoming "fat-stubborn" so it won't waste any heat. So when you only eat a couple of times a day, your body will store as much food as it can (much of it being fat) and will hold on to as much bodyfat as it can. This prevents you from getting lean and spoils your ability to boost your serotonin levels.

What you need to do is "graze," trying to spread out your meals throughout the day. So instead of eating 2–3 large meals eat 5–6 smaller meals. This gives your body a constant supply of nutrients for repair and muscle growth as well as stabilizes insulin and blood sugar levels. You do not want to eat by accident or only when you are hungry. By the time your body tells you it needs food, your metabolism has slowed down and has already been burning protein for energy.

Remember, a meal does not have to be four courses. It can simply be a piece of fruit with cottage cheese, a tuna fish sandwich (low fat mayo), or a meal replacement bar or shake.

#2–Focus On Portions, Not Calories

It can be hard enough trying to eat quality foods, much less having to count grams. A much easier approach is to use the palm of your hand or a clenched fist to determine the amount of food you should eat at each meal. Eating 4–6 fist-sized portions of quality protein and carbohydrates is all you need to worry about during your *40-40-20 Solution*. Each fist-size portion should be around 25–35 grams of protein and carbohydrates. Experiment and find out how many meals you need to eat to get the appropriate amount of protein and carbohydrates in relation to your bodyweight. Again, don't worry about the fat too much. We will go over how you can get the appropriate amount and type of fat in the EFA and Omega-3 Solution section.

#3–Feed Your Mind and Body with Quality Foods

Just as we discussed building a house at the beginning of this chapter, certain foods have specific functions. You need to know what purpose each piece of material is suited for and how and when to put each piece in its proper place. You need the proper materials to construct and repair your muscles, brain cells, hormones, and neurotransmitters and this comes from consistently feeding your body with the right type of foods.

With this in mind, here is the list of the nutrient-rich *40-40-20 Solution* Power Foods that will help your body recover from your workouts and put you on the way to getting you in shape and *Feeling Good for Life*.

40-40-20 Solution **Power Foods**

Proteins	Carbohydrates	Vegetables
Salmon	Sweet Potato	Broccoli
Tuna	Yam	Lettuce
Cottage Cheese	Baked Potato	Tomatoes
Milk	Spaghetti	Avocado
Chicken Breast	Oatmeal	Spinach
Turkey Breast	Brown and Wild Rice	Mushrooms
Egg Whites	Beans (Black, Pinto, Navy)	Cauliflower
Egg Substitutes	Corn	Asparagus
Lean Beef	Fat-free Yogurt	Celery
Lean Sirloin or Steak	Whole-wheat Bread	Cucumbers
Ostrich	Lentils	Peas
Shrimp	Apple	Carrots
Lobster	Orange	Brussels Sprouts
Fat Free Cheese	Strawberries	Chili
Crab	Watermelon	Onion
Lean Ham	Barley	Olives
Tofu	Pumpkin	Green and Red Peppers
Soy	Low Fat/Sugar Ice Cream	Squash

Choose one fist size portion of protein and carbohydrates for a *40-40-20 Solution* meal. Eat at least 2–3 portions of vegetables each day

#4–Drink 8–10 Glasses of Water a Day

In addition to your *40-40-20 Solution* meals, you need to hydrate your body with an adequate supply of water. Water serves as the major transporter of nutrients, hormones, neurotransmitters, waste products, and antibodies throughout the body. It also plays an important role in cellular activity, regulates the acid-base balance of our bodies, and serves as a temperature regulator via perspiration.

During exercise you can lose up to 1 liter of water per hour and if you fail to rehydrate yourself, it can lead to sluggishness and cramps.

Therefore, you should drink a glass of water before, during, and after you exercise. Never wait until you are thirsty to drink water because by that time, you are already dehydrated. It is also a good idea to drink at least one glass of water with each meal to aid with absorption.

#5–Don't Be Afraid to Splurge One Day a Week

Even though you have a variety of great tasting foods to choose from in the list of *40-40-20 Solution* Power Foods, there are going to be times when you crave something sweet or fatty. Having these cravings is perfectly natural and you can actually use these cravings to your advantage.

There is both a physiological and psychological benefit to eating whatever you want once a week. Our bodies sometimes biologically crave certain foods, so splurging can get rid of these hunger pangs by provide your body with something it is asking for. Psychologically, you may come to a point where you feel deprived of the foods you used to eat. This perceived feeling of a loss of choice can be relieved by a day of not worrying about what you are eating. You can see the free day as a way of treating yourself. Since you have reasonably adhered to your *Nutrition-4-Life* Diet for the week, you are giving yourself a reward for all your hard work.

It is unrealistic to think that you are going to eat perfectly for the rest of your life. If you think like this, you are setting yourself up for failure. Obviously you do not want to go overboard, but don't restrain yourself too much on your free days either. Enjoy yourself and don't be afraid to satisfy that urge at the end of the week.

#6–Don't Eat Before or After Working Out

If you can, try performing your *Feeling Good for Life* Aerobic Solution first thing in the morning on an empty stomach. You see, after your body has fasted and stored all its carbohydrates during the night your body is more apt to burn fat for fuel during a morning *Feeling Good for Life* Aerobic Solution. This increased breakdown in fat will mean extra tryptophan going to your brain to make more serotonin. If you cannot perform your *Feeling Good for Life* Aerobic Solution in the morning, make sure to wait at least 2 hours after you eat. As I said before, when your insulin levels are elevated, it prevents you from breaking down fat, so if you eat a bagel or candy bar before your *Feeling Good for Life* Aerobic Solution, you will use carbohydrates for fuel instead of fat. Waiting two hours will allow your insulin levels to stabilize so you can break down more fat during your *Feeling Good for Life* Aerobic Solution.

You are also going to want to wait 45 minutes to an hour to eat after your *Feeling Good for Life* Aerobic Solution. There is about an hour "fat-burning window" after you work out that you can use to get the most out of your *Feeling Good for Life* Aerobic Solution. After your workout, you are still going to be burning calories and fat, especially after an intense *Feeling Good for Life* Aerobic Solution, and if you eat right after your workout you are going to raise your insulin levels and disrupt this fat-burning opportunity. Wait about 45 minutes to an hour after you workout to eat.

#7–Eat Big After Your *Feeling Good for Life* Weight Training Solution

After a good *Feeling Good for Life* Weight Training Solution workout, your muscles are screaming for you to replace the fuel you have used up. This is a perfect time to consume a large meal high in protein and carbohydrates so you can elicit a strong insulin response to drive into your muscles the essential nutrients you depleted during your workout. This may seem confusing since I have been telling you that you need to stabilize insulin levels and not raise them too much. Well, this is the one time that it is acceptable to increase your insulin levels.

After your *Feeling Good for Life* Weight Training Solution, your muscle cells are hypersensitive to insulin and carbohydrates because they want to replenish all the glucose and amino acids that were used during your workout. So when you raise your insulin levels with a high amount of protein and carbohydrates, they will go directly into your muscle cells instead of fat cells. This will promote the replacement of glycogen in your muscles and jump-start the recovery process by increasing protein synthesis. A good meal replacement shake high in protein and simple sugars that is in line with the *40-40-20 Solution* taken within an hour of your *Feeling Good for Life* Weight Training Solution will do the trick.

#8–Shop for Groceries in the *40-40-20 Solution* Frame of Mind

One of the best ways to integrate this new way of eating into your life is to make sure that your refrigerator and shelves are stocked with *40-40-20 Solution* Power Foods. It will be much easier for you to follow the *40-40-20 Solution* if you have an abundance of these foods and little junk food available. Also, don't ever go shopping when you are hungry. If you do so, you will be tempted to get things that are not good for you, making it harder for you to stick to your *40-40-20* Solution. So try to stock up on a variety of quality sources of protein, carbohydrates, and vegetables from the list of *40-40-20 Solution* Power Foods that you will enjoy eating.

The EFA and Omega-3 Solution

Under the category of unsaturated fats, there is a group of special fats that you are going to make a conscious effort to consume more of during your *Nutrirtion-4-Life* Diet and these are the Essential fatty acids (EFAs). Essential means that your body cannot produce them on its own, so you must get them from the food you eat. Essential fatty acids can be divided into two categories: omega-3 and omega-6 fatty acids.

Essential fatty acids are an essential component of the human diet, but over the past century the American diet has changed dramatically, greatly reducing the amount of essential fatty acids we ingest. Before the 20th Century, essential fatty acids were common elements in our diet because we ate more cold-water fish from the ocean and lakes, more wild animals, and fewer processed foods. These dietary changes are largely responsible for the prevalence of chronic illnesses and widespread obesity.

Both of these essential fatty acids are necessary for the structural integrity of our cell membranes and are the building blocks for hormones that regulate most of our essential biological functions. Essential fatty acids play an important role in immune system response, testosterone production, and proper brain health and development. Research has also shown that people who are depressed have low levels of omega-3 fatty acids and supplementation with omega-3 fatty acids improves depression. It is thought that the lack of omega-3 fatty acids in the diet combined with an excess of saturated fats can lead to the formation of brain cell membranes that are much less fluid and pliable than normal. This causes disruptions in these cells ability to control major functions, such as signal transmission between cells, conversion of food for usable energy, and the making of valuable neurotransmitters like serotonin. Also, omega-3 fatty acids play a critical role in controlling insulin activity by slowing down the rate of carbohydrates that are digested and enter your bloodstream. Ironically, consuming omega-3 fatty acids actually enables you to tap into your stored body fat for energy.

Powerful Prostaglandins

A major function of EFAs is the production of the special hormone-like compounds called eicosanoids. When we eat omega-3 and omega-6 fatty acids, they are either incorporated directly into our cell membranes or converted into eicosanoids. These eicosanoids are made up of many different classes of cell-signaling molecules called prostaglandins. Prostaglandins are involved in a number of metabolic functions, such as inflammation, nerve transmission, blood pressure, cholesterol levels, and heart function.

There are both good and bad prostaglandins and the type of EFAs you consume determines which prostaglandins you create. Omega-6 fatty acids produce both good and bad prostaglandins whereas omega-3 fatty acids only produce the good prostaglandins. When these prostaglandins are in balance, you are at optimal mental and physical health, but when they are out of whack, you can have serious problems. So the key to begin *Feeling*

Good for Life is to try to get more omega-3 fatty acids in your diet to balance out the bad prostaglandins produced by the omega-6 fatty acids. A fat intake of about 20% that is high in omega-3 fatty acids and in line with the *40-40-20 Solution* will optimize your ability to produce good prostaglandins and stabilize insulin levels to burn more fat and boost serotonin levels.

You should try to consume from 3–5 grams of omega-3 fatty acids a day. You can get this from your daily food or from omega-3 supplements. Cold-water fish such as salmon, mackerel, and trout are the best sources of omega-3 fatty acids. Freshwater fish and fish from lakes can be contaminated with many chemicals. They also tend to have lower concentrations of omega-3 fatty acids. You can also get omega-3 fatty acids from pecans and walnuts. A tablespoon of flaxseed oil or a serving of omega-3 gel supplements 2–3 times a day with meals will also give you all the EFAs you need to begin *Feeling Good for Life.*

Alpha Lipoic Acid—The Insulin Stabilizer/Serotonin Booster

Often referred to as the "universal antioxidant," alpha lipoic acid is an amazing vitamin-like compound that is a coenzyme for numerous metabolic reactions throughout our body. It plays a major role in protecting our cells, producing energy, and best of all, can increase serotonin levels. Alpha lipoic acid can be found in small amounts in your body, but supplementation with alpha lipoic acid has been shown to provide a multitude of mental and physical benefits.

Quite possibly, you have heard of free radicals and how they can adversely affect our health. Free radicals are byproducts produced during metabolic reactions involving oxygen. It is quite ironic that we cannot live without oxygen, but when you utilize oxygen in a metabolic reaction, it produces these chemicals that are damaging to your health. Alpha lipoic acid seeks out these free radicals and destroys them so they can't cause damage to your cells. First, alpha lipoic acid gets rid of free radicals through a "duel" antioxidant effect. Most vitamins are either water soluble or fat soluble, but alpha lipoic acid is both, which means that alpha lipoic acid can fight free radicals outside of your cells as well as pass through the lipid bilayer (your cell membrane made out of fatty acids) and do its job inside the cell. Secondly, alpha lipoic acid recycles other powerful antioxidants such as vitamin C and E, extending their life so they can scavenge for free radicals for a longer period of time.

The other powerful property of alpha lipoic acid is that it heavily influences the conversion of sugar into energy for our cells to use. First, alpha lipoic acid enhances the uptake of glucose into your muscle cells and inhibits glycosglation, an abnormal binding of sugar to protein. It then helps your mitochondria, powerful structures responsible for energy production inside every muscle cell, produce the main source of fuel for your body, adenosine tri phosphate (ATP). Alpha lipoic acid also increases insulin sensitivity in muscle cells, which means that your muscle are more responsive to insulin, resulting in more glucose and amino acids traveling into the cells with the use of less insulin. In fact, alpha lipoic acid is so good at improving insulin levels that it has been used in Europe for years as a treatment for diabetes. So what does this mean for you? You know all the bad things that can happen when insulin levels are too high. Well, alpha lipoic acid can help your cells get the nutrients they need by using insulin more efficiently. This means more fat being burned, less desire to eat carbohydrates, and increased serotonin levels.

Remember that the amount of serotonin you make is dependent on how much tryptophan enters your brain, so increasing tryptophan will increase serotonin levels. People who are depressed tend to have low levels of both serotonin and tryptophan. Alpha lipoic can make tryptophan more available to enter the brain to produce more serotonin. The influx of tryptophan into the brain is dependent on whether it is in free form or bound to albumin therefore, the more free form tryptophan, the more serotonin.

Another barrier to tryptophan entering the brain is other amino acids called Large Neutral Amino Acids (LNAAs) trying to get into the brain. If there are too many LNAAs, then tryptophan has a hard time getting into the brain. Alpha lipoic acid helps insulin drive all these amino acids into your muscles cells except tryptophan. Tryptophan does not get transported along with the LNAAs because it is bound to the protein albumin, preventing it from being taken into the muscle cell. This means more tryptophan is available in the bloodstream to out compete with the LNAAs in getting into the brain. And don't forget: when you breakdown fat during your *Feeling Good for Life* Exercise Solution, you are going to unbind tryptophan and cause even more to go into the brain to make serotonin.

Super Vitamins

A Multi a Day Keeps the Blues Away

Plain and simple, you should take a multivitamin each day. It is difficult to get all the vitamins and minerals you need through your daily food intake, even if you are following the *40-40-20 Solution*. The recommended daily allowances (RDA) are inadequate, especially for people who are exercising. These guidelines were set up to prevent deficiencies, not for people who are active. Therefore, you should try to get more then what is recommended. Make sure that your multivitamin is low in calcium because calcium inhibits the absorption of many other vitamins and minerals. Calcium is not bad, especially for women trying to prevent osteoporosis, just take a calcium supplement at a separate time.

B Vitamins

Deficiencies in B vitamins (B_1, B_2, B_3, B_5, B_6, and B_{12}) have been associated with numerous health problems, such as abnormal carbohydrate, fat and protein metabolism, reduced functioning of the nervous system and digestive tract, dysregulation of blood cell formation, and depression. People with poor diets (which is very common in people with depression) are at risk for deficiencies in the B-complex vitamins. Supplementation with B vitamins has been shown to help brain cells function properly and reduce depression by increasing serotonin levels. A good B-complex from your local drug store should do the trick.

Folic Acid

Folic acid deficiency is the most common vitamin deficiency in the world and folic acid levels have been consistently demonstrated to be extremely low in people with depression. Supplementation with folic acid increases serotonin levels and improves mood. Shoot for 1 gram of folic acid a day.

Vitamin C

Vitamin C is a powerful antioxidants that supports the immune system, helps heals cuts, burns, and broken bones, repairs your ligaments and tendons, reduces free radial damage and increases the absorption of important vitamins and minerals such as iron and folic acid. A deficiency in vitamin C can lead to scurvy, loss of energy, swollen or painful joints, and depression. Vitamin C is not toxic, unless taken in excessive amounts such as 10 grams. People who are exercising and feeling blue should take 1–2 grams of vitamin C in doses of 250–500mg.

Vitamin E

Vitamin E is also a strong antioxidant that protects our cellular membranes from oxidative damage, recycles vitamin C, protects against various cancers, improves insulin sensitivity, and helps athletes recover from strenuous workouts. Deficiencies if vitamin E can result in loss of energy, lack of concentration, and a decrease in nerve function. You should not take more than 1,500 IU of the natural d-form of vitamin E. Take about 800–1,000 IU per day.

CHAPTER 5

Taking Action with *Feeling Good for Life*

Your Troubles Will Cease to Exist Once You Make the Decision to Change

Whenever I talk to a friend or client about a problem they have, I always make it a point to share with them my attitude toward personal problems and how that mindset influences the way I live my life. Do you know what I believe a problem is? It is simply a point where a decision needs to be made. The problem that is causing you so much distress and sadness will cease to exist once you make the decision to change and do something about the situation. With very few exceptions, I don't believe there are such things as problems. If you are not doing well in school, you have to make the decision to study more. If a valuable relationship is on the rocks, you have to decide to make the effort to work things out. If you need to lose weight, you have to decide to start exercising and eat better. If you are feeling depressed, you have to make the decision to either seek professional help or use *Feeling Good for Life*. This conscious decision to change is usually the harder choice, and that is why so few people follow this path.

Of course, deciding to take control of your life by utilizing the natural medicines found in your body can be more difficult when you are feeling down in the dumps. So how can you make this decision to change if your thoughts are distorted with feelings of sadness and gloom? The answer is to use clinically tested motivational and adherence techniques that will not only help you make the conscious decision to change your life, but also show you powerful solutions to the obstacles you may face on your journey to better mental and physical health. In this chapter we are going to bring together everything you have learned and lay a foundation for staying on course in getting in shape and begin *Feeling Good for Life*.

The decision to take control of your emotional and physical health is a monumental step. However, this decision to take control does not happen just because you think it. It requires that you have a plan but more importantly, that you take action. You will not receive any of the wonderful benefits from *Feeling Good for Life* if you just sit and think about exercising and eating healthy. If you are like most people, you have probably started an exercise program or diet many times before, only to slide right back to where you first began. Well, this time is going to be different. This time you are going to succeed! You have come this far in reading about the wonderful benefits that come from *Feeling Good for Life*, now it is time to apply that knowledge by getting you motivated to take that initial step. Come on, let's make it happen!

Recognizing Why the Decision Must be Made

Our lives are full of decisions and the greater the impact a specific decision will have on our life, the more time and energy we spend contemplating that decision. Small decision, such as deciding what to eat for breakfast may only take a minute, whereas a life-changing decision, such as moving to a new city or buying your first house requires a great deal of thought and planning. Unfortunately, most people put exercise and healthy eating into this "small" decision category. They do not see it as a decision that *must* take place. What I want to do is show you one more time that beginning *Feeling Good for Life* is a decision you need to make and there is no logical reason why you shouldn't start as soon as you put this book down. We will do this by using the *Feeling Good for Life* Balance Sheet.

Right now you may be thinking to yourself, "*Feeling Good for Life* can't help me," or "Exercise and healthy eating is not going to make that much of a difference." To combat these negative thoughts we are going to use the *Feeling Good for Life* Balance Sheet to give you a concrete document that lists all the amazing benefits you will gain during your *Feeling Good for Life* Experience. So take a moment to list all the advantages and disadvantages that will come from using *Feeling Good for Life*. Be as specific as possible. It may be helpful to refer to the previous chapters and review all the benefits we have discussed. Don't restrict the list to only the psychological benefits. Include all the physical and social benefits as well.

Feeling Good for Life Balance Sheet

Benefits (Advantages)	Costs (Disadvantages)

Once you have completed the task, look at each side of the balance sheet. What is the most prominent feature you see on the list? Can you believe how much longer the list in the left column is compared to the right column? This is because *Feeling Good for Life* has the power to provide you with a multitude of mental and physical health benefits that can change your life forever. Now let's go on and set out exactly how you will experience all these benefits.

Setting Your Goals

It is now time to create a roadmap by writing down in detail what you want to achieve during your *Feeling Good for Life* Experience. It is always difficult to reach your final destination without knowing the exact path you need to take. This is why I am going to guide you through the process of writing down your goals. I want you to have something to refer to that will help you focus your energy toward accomplishing your goals.

Start by dividing your goals into long-term and short-term goals. Your long-term goals are going to be what you ultimately want to accomplish out of *Feeling Good for Life*. After you have decided this, you will get more specific by setting short-term goals that will guide you in achieving your long-term goals. By setting small, manageable goals you will allow yourself to focus on what you need to accomplish in the near future, rather than focusing on something that is too far ahead.

It is also necessary for you to be as descriptive as possible about your goals. It will do you no good if you are vague and abstract. You can say, "I want to increase my aerobic fitness," or "I want to eat better," but it will be more beneficial to say, "I will complete at least 20 minutes of exercise, 3 days a week, for the next 4 weeks," or "I am going to start eating 4 meals a day this week and 5 meals a day next week." Being detailed about your goals focuses your actions and leaves no room for excuses.

Make sure you set flexible, realistic goals instead of fixed, rigid ones. It is understandable that you may set lofty goals because you are motivated and want to get the most out of your *Feeling Good for Life* Experience, but if they are unrealistic, you will be setting yourself up for failure. You must allow yourself to work within your own capabilities to achieve the mental and physical improvements brought about from *Feeling Good for Life*.

Feeling Good for Life Goal Setting

Long-Term Goals

What do I want to achieve out of *Feeling Good for Life*?

Short-Term Goals

What are the intermediate goals I need to achieve to reach my long-term goals?

Daily Goals

What do I have to do on a daily basis to achieve my short-term goals? Write down at least two things that you need to accomplish each day.

Relapse Prevention: How to Stick to Your Goals

You have been using *Feeling Good for Life* for a few weeks now and things have been going great. You have not missed a workout, you are eating healthy, losing fat, and beginning to feel good for the first time in months. Then something unexpected happens that seriously disrupts your life. You may get injured, an important relationship may end, or you may get called away on a long business trip. How are you going deal with such events so they don't prevent you from continuing on with *Feeling Good for Life?*

The first step in preventing these types of events from leading you off course is to accept the fact that difficult situations are going to arise from time to time. It is not a matter of whether these things will happen, but how and when they will happen. You just have to make sure that when they occur, you don't think all is lost. More importantly, there are things you can do to counteract the negative effects brought about by these situations.

First let's stop and think about any possible high-risk situations you may encounter during your *Feeling Good for Life* Experience that may cause you to stop exercising, such as vacations or out-of-town business trips. It will benefit you greatly if you find ways to cope with these potential setbacks, such as planning walks or runs while on these trips. Try to consider any obstacles that you may face and think of ways you can prevent these situations from interfering with your *Feeling Good for Life* Exercise Solution or *Nutrition-4-Life* Diet.

Also, it is good to set flexible goals to allow you to work around unpredictable events in your life. Too many people see unavoidable disruptions in their lives as a failure on their part and blame themselves. In reality, disruptions happen to everyone. Just because you miss a workout or go off your diet does not mean that you have failed. It just means that you have strayed off your path and need to regroup and get back on the right track. If you are flexible within your *Feeling Good for Life* Exercise Solution and *Nutrition-4-Life* Diet goals, disruptions can be avoided or handled with little stress. Although you are unable to predict all the setbacks that may arise, by using the *Feeling Good for Life* Relapse Prevention Sheet you can help prevent most of the events that can cause you to relapse during your *Feeling Good for Life* Experience.

Feeling Good for Life Relapse Prevention Sheet

*What are possible setbacks that I may encounter during my *Feeling Good for Life* Exercise Solution?

*What types of strategies can I use to cope with these setbacks?

Relapse Coping

*What were the triggering events of my relapse?

*What did I do right?

*What mistakes did I make?

*What do I need to do differently next time?

Record Your Progress

It is not enough to state your goals and how you plan to achieve them. You also need to keep track of your progress every step of the way. This is why you are going to routinely check if you are accomplishing your goals and keep track of your progress with the *Feeling Good for Life* Journal and the *Feeling Good for Life* Exercise Solution Progress Sheets in appendix D and E. By measuring your progress you can stay focused and make sure you are achieving what you set out to do during your *Feeling Good for Life* Experience. If you run out of these Progress Sheets, you can also print them off www.*FeelingGoodforLife*.com. Please don't underestimate the power of these valuable tools. The more time you invest in *Feeling Good for Life*, the greater your chances in making exercise and quality nutrition a regular part of your life.

Putting It All Together—The *Feeling Good for Life* Contract

How many times have you heard people promise themselves that they are going to go on a diet or start an exercise program? Now how many people do you actually see follow through with these self-promises? The difference between people thinking and actually doing is quite disheartening. It is estimated that only 12 to 22 % of adults in the United States get recommended levels of exercise and even when people do begin to exercise, they find it difficult to stick to their program. In fact, about 50 % of people drop out of a structured exercise program within the first 6 months. These people all start out intending to stick to their goals, but can't keep up with them—often because they don't have the knowledge or know-how needed to continue.

You have the knowledge from the past 4 chapters, now I am going to help you make the final commitment needed to take charge of your life. The *Feeling Good for Life* Contract is the final tool on your journey to getting in shape and becoming depression free for life. By using the *Feeling Good for Life* Contract, you are signing a concrete document that shows that you have made a personal commitment to honor all the self-promises you have made in this chapter and to begin and finish *Feeling Good for Life*. This written agreement specifies what your *Feeling Good for Life* Exercise Solution and *Nutrition-4-Life* goals are and what you have to do

to achieve them. Take your time to make sure that you agree to what is
stated in the contract. Then sign it and ask another person to witness it.

Feeling Good for Life Contract

I _____ agree to accomplish the following:

1) To attend all of my *Feeling Good for Life* Exercise Solution sessions I
schedule with a minimum of _____ times per week for a total of _____
weeks.

2) To eat at least _____ meals a day with a food composition of the *40-40-20
Solution*.

3) If for any reason I miss an exercise session due to illness or any other
unavoidable circumstance, I will make up the session by (specify)_____

_____

4) If I accomplish the goals of attending all my scheduled sessions and eat
reasonably well, I will reward myself at the end of each week in the following
manner:_____

_____

5) If I do not accomplish these goals, I will deprive myself of the following:

_____

Signed:

_____   _____
(Participant)   (Date)

_____   _____
(Witness)   (Date)

Final Tips for Your *Feeling Good for Life* Experience

Don't Believe In the All or Nothing Principle

At some point during *Feeling Good for Life* you will probably skip an exercise session or go off your diet. This is normal. The key is to not to see it as the end of the world. For example, if someone is on a strict diet and takes a bite out a piece of pie, cake, or some other dessert, they feel as if they have self-destructed. That person thinks, "I have failed at my diet so I might as well eat the whole piece of dessert." This "all or nothing" mentality is destructive because you think that if you have failed just a little bit, you have completely failed so you might as well give up. The same thing holds for your *Feeling Good for Life* Exercise Solution and *Nutrition-4-Life* Diet. Just because you missed a workout or ate that piece of pie does not mean that you should give up on *Feeling Good for Life*. You have to get back in the saddle and start where you left off. Relapse is a normal part of life. You have to learn that it is not the end of the world and make sure that it does not take your life down the wrong path.

Seek Social Support

Seeking out people's support during your *Feeling Good for Life* Experience can greatly improve your attitude and help your motivation. There is nothing wrong with asking people to consistently encourage you to exercise regularly and stick to your diet. It can also be a good idea to invite friends or family to exercise with you or possibly join a group of people who exercise regularly. Having people around you who exercise on a regular basis can inspire you to exercise more as well as provide you with good role models.

Make Sure to Choose Exercises and Foods You Enjoy

Your *Feeling Good for Life* Experience will be much more pleasurable if you participate in exercises you enjoy and eat foods you like. Your motivation to exercise and stick to your diet will soon start to fade if you are not enjoying yourself. Find one or two exercises that you enjoy and have a variety of foods you can choose from. If you get bored with one form of exercise or certain foods, experiment and change things a little. You can add variety to your exercise routine by changing the pace of your aerobic exercise every other workout or if you are lifting weights, change the order of your weight training routine.

Set an Exercise Schedule

Committing yourself to a consistent time to exercise can help you strengthen the habit of working out. If you make exercise a priority in your life, you will increase the chances of sticking to the goals you set out earlier in the chapter. A great time to exercise is early in the morning. If you exercise late in the afternoon, you may be tempted to miss your workout because you are tired or you may schedule something else in place of your exercise session. Morning exercise may also put you in a good mood because you have achieved one of your goals early in the day. If you can't exercise in the morning, set time aside solely for the purpose of exercise.

Don't Overtrain

As we discussed in chapter 2, if you exercise too much there is a chance that you can actually make yourself feel worse than you were feeling before you started *Feeling Good for Life*. If you overtrain, you may begin to feel tired and your symptoms may start to resurface. It is good to begin with mild to moderate exercise and gradually build up to your exercise goals. If you start feeling bad again, take a few days off from exercising to allow yourself some rest and recuperation.

Continue to Reward Yourself

Don't forget to consistently reward yourself when you accomplish your goals. If at the end of the week you have accomplished your short-term goals and reasonably adhered to your *Feeling Good for Life* Exercise Solution and *Nutrition-4-Life* Diet, treat yourself to dinner and a movie or buy yourself something new. As you progress through your *Feeling Good for*

Life Experience, keep rewarding yourself for accomplishing your long-term goals as well. Rewarding yourself will reinforce the idea that exercise and proper nutrition is a good behavior in your life.

Support Yourself With Positive Reinforcement

You may sometimes have negative feelings about exercise and healthy eating. This is normal and should not make you panic. Instead of thinking to yourself, "I am not looking forward to exercising today," turn those negative thoughts into positive self-talk such as, "I know that exercising is very important and I will feel great after I am done." This positive self-reinforcement can help when you reach a sticking point. By making a conscious effort to think positively, you can make a big difference in your motivation and increase your chances of staying on track.

Continue to Learn More About Exercise

You will benefit greatly from taking an interest in learning all you can about exercise. Knowledge is power and it will motivate you when you learn more about the nature of exercise. Good sources of information about exercise can be found in publications by the American College of Sports Medicine, Human Kinetics, or by asking qualified exercise leaders, such as *certified* personal trainers and fitness instructors.

Feeling Good for Life

My main goal for *Feeling Good for Life* is to teach as many people as I can how to release the powerful and miraculous self-cures that lie inside all of us so that any sadness people feel can move aside and joy and happiness can enter their lives. In the past 5 chapters I have given you the tools and knowledge that will help you on your way to getting in the best shape of your life and becoming depression free. You now have a decision to make: you can continue to allow yourself to stay in your emotional abyss or take control of your life by using the only therapy that will burn fat, build muscle, boost your mood, and conquer your depression. You know what the only choice is—to begin *Feeling Good for Life.*

Appendixes

Appendix A

Goldberg Depression Scale

The diagnosis and treatment of depression and other psychiatric disorders requires trained medical professionals. The information provided below is to be used for educational purposes only. It should NOT be used as a substitute for seeking professional care for the diagnosis and treatment of any medical/psychiatric disorder. The potential risks associated with improper diagnosis or treatment can only be minimized by consultations with mental health professionals. Physicians should check standard medical texts, for dosages, indications and contraindications, prior to prescribing any drug.

By: Ivan Goldberg

Instructions: You might reproduce this scale and use it on a weekly basis to track your moods. It also might be used to show your doctor how your symptoms have changed from one visit to the next. Changes of five or more points are significant. This scale is not designed to make a diagnosis of depression or take the place of a professional diagnosis. If you suspect that you are depressed, please consult with a mental health professional as soon as possible.

The items below refer to how you have felt and behaved during the past week. For each item, indicate the extent to which it is true, by circling one of the numbers that follows it. Using the following scale:

0 = Not at all 1 = Just a little 2 = Somewhat
3 = Moderately 4 = Quite a lot 5 = Very much

---

1. I do things slowly.   0 1 2 3 4 5

2. My future seems hopeless.   0 1 2 3 4 5

3. It is hard for me to concentrate on reading.   0 1 2 3 4 5

4. The pleasure and joy has gone out of my life.   0 1 2 3 4 5

5. I have difficulty making decisions.   0 1 2 3 4 5

6. I have lost interest in aspects of life that
    used to be important to me.   0 1 2 3 4 5

7. I feel sad, blue, and unhappy.   0 1 2 3 4 5

8. I am agitated and keep moving around.   0 1 2 3 4 5

9. I feel fatigued.   0 1 2 3 4 5

10. It takes great effort for me to do
    simple things.   0 1 2 3 4 5

11. I feel that I am a guilty person who deserves
    to be punished.   0 1 2 3 4 5

12. I feel like a failure.   0 1 2 3 4 5

13. I feel lifeless...more dead than alive.   0 1 2 3 4 5

14. My sleep has been disturbed...too little,
    too much, or broken sleep.   0 1 2 3 4 5

15. I spend time thinking about HOW I might
    kill myself.   0 1 2 3 4 5

16. I feel trapped or caught.   0 1 2 3 4 5

17. I feel depressed even when good things
    happen to me.   0 1 2 3 4 5

18. Without trying to diet, I have lost, or
    gained, weight.   0 1 2 3 4 5

                                        Total Score_____

SCORES:

54 and up: Severely Depressed

36–53: Moderate—Severe

22–35: Mild—Moderate

18–21: Borderline depression

10–17: Possibly Mildly Depressed

0–9: No Depression Likely

This is not meant as a diagnosis tool!

If you are suffering from feelings that are causing you concern and interfere with your daily functioning or if you are having thoughts of killing yourself or someone else, you should seek immediate treatment from a trained mental health professional within your community!

Copyright (c) 1993 Ivan Goldberg

What is Depressive Disorder?

A depressive disorder is an illness that involves the body, mood, and thoughts. It affects the way a person eats and sleeps, the way one feels about oneself, and the way one thinks about things. A depressive disorder is not the same as a passing blue mood. It is not a sign of personal weakness or a condition that can be willed or wished away. People with a depressive illness cannot merely "pull themselves together" and get better. Without treatment, symptoms can last for weeks, months, or years. Appropriate treatment, however, can help most people who suffer from depression.

Types of Depression

Depressive disorders come in different forms, just as is the case with other illnesses such as heart disease. This pamphlet briefly describes three of the most common types of depressive disorders. However, within these types there are variations in the number of symptoms, their severity, and persistence.

Major depression is manifested by a combination of symptoms (see symptom list) that interfere with the ability to work, study, sleep, eat, and enjoy once pleasurable activities. Such a disabling episode of depression may occur only once but more commonly occurs several times in a lifetime.

A less severe type of depression, dysthymia, involves long-term, chronic symptoms that do not disable, but keep one from functioning well or from feeling good. Many people with dysthymia also experience major depressive episodes at some time in their lives.

Symptoms of Depression

- Persistent sad, anxious, or "empty" mood
- Feelings of hopelessness, pessimism
- Feelings of guilt, worthlessness, helplessness
- Loss of interest or pleasure in hobbies and activities that were once enjoyed, including sex
- Decreased energy, fatigue, being "slowed down"
- Difficulty concentrating, remembering, making decisions

- Insomnia, early-morning awakening, or oversleeping
- Appetite and/or weight loss or overeating and weight gain
- Thoughts of death or suicide; suicide attempts
- Restlessness, irritability
- Persistent physical symptoms that do not respond to treatment, such as headaches, digestive disorders, and chronic pain

This brochure is a new version of the 1994 edition of Plain Talk About Depression and was written by Margaret Strock, Information Resources and Inquiries Branch, Office of Communications and Public Liaison, National Institute of Mental Health (NIMH). Expert assistance was provided by Raymond DePaulo, MD, Johns Hopkins School of Medicine; Ellen Frank, MD, University of Pittsburgh School of Medicine; Jerrold F. Rosenbaum, MD, Massachusetts General Hospital; Matthew V. Rudorfer, MD, and Clarissa K. Wittenberg, NIMH staff members. Lisa D. Alberts, NIMH staff member, provided editorial assistance.

This publication is in the public domain and may be used and reprinted without permission.

NIH Publication No. 00-3561
Printed 2000

Updated: September 13, 2001

For information about NIMH and its programs:

NIMH Public Inquiries
6001 Executive Boulevard, Rm. 8184, MSC 9663
Bethesda, MD 20892-9663 U.S.A.
Voice (301) 443-4513; Fax (301) 443-4279
TTY (301) 443-8431
nimhinfo@nih.gov

Appendix B

Feeling Good for Life Exercise Guide

If your goal is to harden up that midsection, broaden your shoulders, and tone your legs, The *Feeling Good for Life* Weight Training Solution is the answer. If you are looking to decrease your bodyfat, weight training combined with aerobic exercise will get you there faster then aerobic exercise alone. As we discussed earlier, your body has to burn more calories to maintaining a pound of muscle then a pound of fat therefore, when you increase ratio of muscle to fat, you will increase your metabolic rate and burn more fat calories throughout the day.

In the follow section, I have included 34 weight training exercise and 9 different stretches you can use to work your entire body. I will first go over all the weight training exercises you can use for your chest, back, shoulders, biceps, triceps, abs, and legs and then I will show you how to stretch all these muscle groups.

To maximize the gains from your *Feeling Good for Life* Weight Training Solution, make sure you perform every exercise as I have described them. As a general rule, take 3–4 seconds to lower the weight and 2–3 to lift the weight. This will insure that you are lifting the weight in a slow, controlled manner. Good luck!

Photos by Marcos Salazar and Rosina Anaya

Chest Exercise

Chest Press Machine

Adjust the seat of the machine so that the handles are aligned with the middle of
your chest. When sitting on the machine, make sure to keep your back straight
and pressed against the pad throughout the entire movement. Grasp the handles
and push the bar forward, making sure not to lock out your elbows at the end of
the movement. Pause for a brief second at full extension, then lower the handles
slowly back to the starting position. Exhale while you push the weight and inhale
when you lower the weight.

*Tip: Don't hunch forward at the end of the movement. Your back and shoulders
should stay on the pad at all times*

Bench Press

Lie down on the bench press and plant your feet firmly on the floor to stabilize your body. Line your eyes up with the bar and grasp it with a slightly wider then shoulders grip. Lift the bar off the rack and slowly lower it to the middle of your chest. At the bottom of the movement, pause for a brief second and then push the bar back up to the starting position. Hold the weight for a second and then repeat the movement. Focus on inhaling while lowering the weight and exhaling as you push the weight up. Make sure not to lock out your arms at the end of the movement to minimize stress on your elbows. Never bounce the bar off your chest just so you can lift more weight.

Tip: Keep your hips and lower back on the bench throughout the entire movement. Push your lower and upper back into the bench as you press the weight up.

Dumbbell Bench Press

Sit down at the edge of a bench holding a pair of
dumbbells on each knee. In one fluid motion, roll
back onto the bench while pushing the dumbbells
up with your knees to a position slightly outside
your shoulders. Proceed to push the weight up by
straightening your arms until the dumbbells are
almost touching. Now slowly lower the dumbbells
downward with your hands moving in a semi-circular
motion. When you feel a slight stretch in your chest
and shoulders, stop the downward movement, pause
for a brief second, and push the weight upward.
Focus on maintaining proper form during the whole
movement. Your arms may shake a bit at first, but as
you practice more, the motion will become smoother.

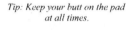

*Tip: Keep your butt on the pad
at all times.*

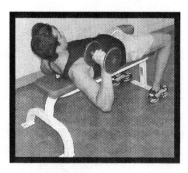

*Tip: There is a tendency to lift your head
up while pushing up the weight. Keep your
head on the bench to prevent neck injuries.*

Dumbbell Incline Press

Sit on an incline press that is elevated to a 35 to 45-degree angle. Lean back with your butt pressed against the pad and your feet planted firmly on the floor. Grip a dumbbell with each hand and place them on your knees. Push the dumbbells up one at a time with your knees, positioning them at the base of your shoulders. Slowly raise the dumbbells until your arms are almost locked out. Lower the weight to the upper part of your chest, concentrating on bringing the dumbbells down in a slow, controlled fashion until you feel a slight stretch. Pause at the bottom for a brief second, then drive the dumbbells back upwards.

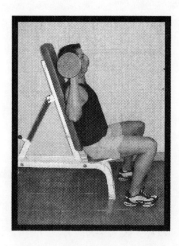

Tip: Don't set the angle of the bench too high. This will cause you to work your shoulders more than your chest.

Dumbbell Fly
(Flat or Incline)

Sit on either a flat bench or an incline
bench that is elevated to a 35 to 45
degree angle. Drive the dumbbells up
in the same manner as the dumbbell
bench or incline press and have your
palms facing each other at the top.
Slowly lower the weights in an arching
motion, keeping your arms slightly bent
during the whole movement. Once you
feel a slight stretch at the bottom, drive
the dumbbells back up through the same
motion.

*Tip: Don't overstretch during the
movement by letting your arms go
below bench level.*

*Tip: Keep a slight bend in your
elbows at all times. Don't straighten
or bend your arms too much.*

Back Exercises

Pulldown

With your hands shoulder width apart, grasp the bar with your palms facing you. Sit with your feet flat on the ground and your upper thighs locked underneath the leg pads to prevent you from bouncing up and down during movement. Slowly pull the bar toward the upper part of your chest while keeping your back arched. Pause for a brief second at the bottom and slowly return the bar to initial position.

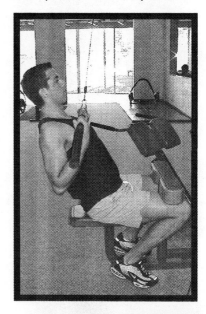

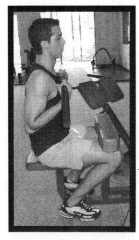

Tip: Do not bend too far forward or backward. It is essential that you keep your back arched and your body stable during the movement. If you don't stay upright or are hunched over, your lats will not contract to their fullest extent.

Machine Back Row

This machine varies from gym to gym, but
the basic principle behind the movement is
the same. Adjust the seat so that the bar is
the same height as the top of your rib cage
and adjust the chest pad so that your arms
are fully extended when you grasp the handles.
Grab hold of the handles and pull the weight
toward your chest. When you cannot pull the
weight back anymore, pause for a second and
return the weight back to the starting position.

*Tip: Make sure not to come off of the chest pad
when you are pulling the weight back. Your body
should stay on the seat and pressed up against
the chest pad throughout the entire movement.*

One Arm Dummbell Row

Place your left hand and left knee on the bench and bend over until your back is flat or parallel to the ground. This position will provide the support needed for your torso during the exercise. Now lower your body to grasp the dumbbell with your right hand, and return your body to the original position. Keeping your back straight, slowly lift the weight up to the side of your torso, making sure your elbow stays close to your side throughout the entire movement. Pause at the top and then lower the weight slowly. When done with the set, repeat with the opposite arm.

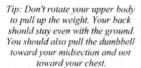

Tip: Don't rotate your upper body to pull up the weight. Your back should stay even with the ground. You should also pull the dumbbell toward your midsection and not toward your chest.

Tip: Don't hunch your back. Keep your head up and your back arched.

Back Extension

Place your ankles under the footrest and lean your upper thighs on the pad. Adjust the setting so that your hipbone is an inch or two above the pad. This will allow enough room for your upper body to bend forward during the exercise. Once you have adjusted the pad, straighten out your body so it makes a straight line, cross your arms across your chest, and slowly lean forward as far as you can while keeping your back straight. Pause at the bottom and then raise your upper body back up the starting position.

Tip: You should not lift your upper body past the straight line made by your body. This will put too much stress on your lower back and could lead to injury.

Shoulder Exercises

Shoulder Press Machine

Adjust the seat height so that the handles are slightly above your shoulders. Keep your back straight and feet on the floor to stabilize your body. Grasp the handles firmly and push the weight up until your elbows are almost fully extended. Pause for a second, then lower the weight slowly back to the starting position. Be sure to exhale while pushing the weight up and inhale while lowering the weight.

Tip: Don't position the seat too high. Your shoulders should not be above the height of the handles.

Dumbbell Shoulder Press

Sit on a bench with your feet on ground, your back
firmly pressed against the pad, and a pair of dumbbells
on your knees. Kick the dumbbells up with your knees
and bring the dumbbells up to slightly above shoulder
height, with your palms facing forward. Press the
dumbbells up until your arms are extended with a
slight bend in the elbow. Pause for a second and
then lower the dumbbells to shoulder height.

*Tip: Your forearms should
be perpendicular to the
floor at all times. Do not
let the dumbbells sway
too far inward or outward.*

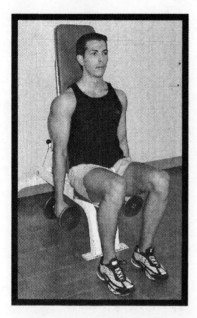 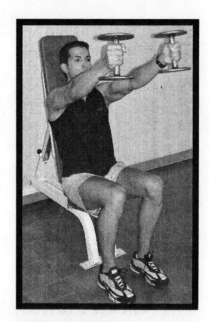

Seated Dumbbell Front Lateral Raise

Sit down on a bench with your back firmly pressed against the pad. Keeping your back straight, slowly raise your arms out in front of you until the dumbbells reach slightly above shoulder height. Pause for a second and then slowly lower your arms back to the starting position..

Tip: Don't bring your arms too far above the head. The dumbbells should stop slightly above shoulder height.

Tip: Don't bring the dumbbells too far back during the exercise. This will cause you to swing the dumbbells and use momentum instead of your shoulders to bring up the weight.

Tip: Don't let your butt move forward so you can lift more weight. Keep your lower back against the pad at all times.

Tip: Don't bring the dumbbells too high up. It is not necessary to go above shoulder height. The higher you raise the dumbbells, the less work your shoulder will be doing during the movement.

Seated Dumbbell Side Lateral Raise

Sit on a bench with your back firmly pressed against the pad. Keeping your back straight, slowly raise your arms out to your sides to slightly above shoulder height. Pause for a second and then slowly lower your arms back to the starting position. This exercise can be done standing, but doing it sitting down against the bench prevents you from swinging your upper body to lift the weight.

Tip: Don't bend your elbows too much or straighten your arms outs completely. You should have a slight bend in the elbow throughout the whole movement.

Dumbbell Shrug

Grasp a dumbbell in each
hand and hold them out at
your sides. Stabilize your
body by sticking your chest
out and arching your back.
Slowly raise your shoulders
back and to your head until
they cannot go any higher.
Pause at the top for a second,
then slowly lower the dumbbells
back to the starting position.

*Tip: Do not hunch your back and let your shoulders move forward during the
movement. Your shoulders should be moving up and slightly back, not forward.
A way to remedy this is to stick your chin in your chest while keeping your chest out.*

Bicep Exercises

Bicep Curl Machine

Adjust the seat height so that you can rest the back of your upper arms comfortably on the arm pad. Place your elbows on the pad about 10-12 inches apart and grasp the handle with an underhand grip. Keeping your upper body stable, curl the weight up as far as possible, pause for a second, and then slowly lower the weight back to the starting position.

Tip: Make sure that you extend all the way down at the starting position and pull up as far as possible at the top.

Barbell Curl

Stand with your knees slightly bent, feet shoulder width apart, and the barbell resting on the front of your thighs. Grasp the bar with your palms facing up and your hands shoulder width apart. With your elbows locked at your sides and your back straight, slowly raise your hands toward your shoulders. Pause at the top to squeeze your biceps, then slowly lower the bar to the starting position.

Tip: Don't take too narrow or too wide of a grip when performing the movement.

Dumbbell Incline Curl

Sit on an incline bench that is elevated to a 35 to 45 degree angle. Lean back with your butt pressed against the pad and your feet planted firmly on the floor. Grasp a dumbbell in each hand and with your upper arm staying perpendicular with the floor, raise the dumbbells up to your shoulders. Pause at the top to contract your biceps, then slowly lower the weight back to the starting position.

Tip: Keep the dumbbells in line with your body. Don't curl the weight out to your sides.

Concentration Curl

Sit on a bench with your feet on the ground and your legs spread apart. Place your upper arm firmly against your inner thigh, bend over while keeping your back straight, and grasp a dumbbell with your palm facing up. Slowly raise your hand toward your chest, making sure to keep your upper arm stable. Pause for a brief second at the top to contract your biceps, then slowly lower the dumbbell to the starting position. Repeat with the opposite arm.

Tip: Don't use your upper body to bring the weight up. Keep your upper arm perpendicular to the floor at all times and your upper body still throughout the whole movement.

Tricep Exercises

Tricep Pushdown

You can perform this exercise with a number of different bars, but for now it is best to pick a straight bar. Attach the bar to the cable and adjust the weight accordingly. Grip the bar with an overhand grip and bring your arms down so that your elbows are close to your body. The bar should be just below your chest when you start the movement. Keeping your elbows locked at your sides, push the handle downward until your arms are fully extended. Hold for a second at full extension and then slowly return the handle to the starting position.

Tip: Don't let your arms rise with the weight. Keep your elbows locked at your sides at all times

Tip: A common mistake is to lean over the handle and push the weight down with your upper body instead of only your triceps. Keep your body erect and only use your triceps to move the weight.

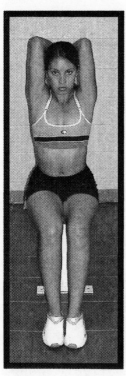

Seated Tricep Extension

Sit on bench with your back straight and feet flat on ground. Grasp a dumbbell with both hands and place it behind your head with your palms facing up. In the starting position, your upper arm should be perpendicular to the floor and your forearms should be bent at a 90-degree angle. Extend your arms so the dumbbell is raised overhead locking out your elbows. Slowly lower dumbbell to initial position and repeat.

Tip: Place the handle between your thumb and forefinger with your palms touching the top of the dumbbell. Don't try grasping the round part of the dumbbell or gripping it with your fingers.

Tip: Don't let your arms flare out. Keep your elbows straight ahead throughout the whole movement.

Lying Dumbbell Extension

Lie down on a flat bench with your
feet firmly planted on the floor and
a dumbbell in each hand. Raise the
dumbbells overhead with your arms
straight and palms facing each other.
Slowly lower the dumbbell toward
your head with your upper arms
bending slightly back. As soon as
you feel a slight stretch in the back
of your arm, extend your arm back
to the starting position. During the
movement, don't let your arms flare
out. They should stay pointed upward
and perpendicular to the ground.

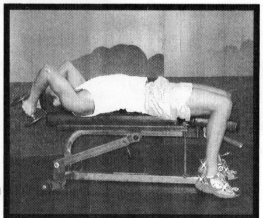

*Tip: Make sure to bring the weight
down far enough and go through the
full range of motion.*

Tricep Kickback

Place your left hand and left knee on the bench and grasp the dumbbell with your right hand. Bend over until your back is flat or parallel to ground. Your upper arm should be aligned with your upper back and should remain like this throughout the entire movement. Keeping your arm parallel with the floor, straighten your arm until it is fully extended. Pause at the top and then lower the dumbbell slowly back to the starting position.

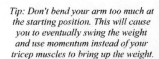

Tip: Don't bend your arm too much at the starting position. This will cause you to eventually swing the weight and use momentum instead of your tricep muscles to bring up the weight.

Tip: Make sure to keep your upper arm parallel with the floor at all times so you can fully contract the triceps.

Ab Exercises

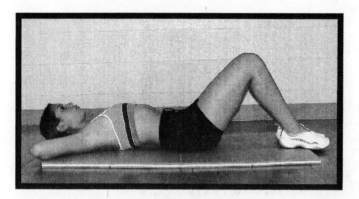

Crunch

Lie on your back with your feet on the floor and your knees bent. Place your hands loosely on the back of your head and begin lifting your shoulders and torso off the floor, tightening your abdominal muscles to accomplish this. Pause at the top and squeeze your abs, then return your torso to the floor in a slow controlled manner. Make sure you are using your abdominals to lift yourself up. Don't use your arms to jerk your head and torso off the floor. This can cause injury to your neck and should be avoided.

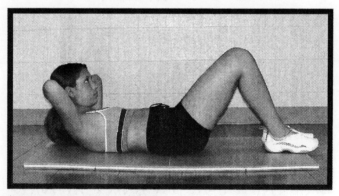

Tip: You should not bring your torso off the floor as if you are doing a sit up. Your lower back should stay on the floor during the whole exercise. The crunch has a very short range of motion and once you bring your upper body up too much, your abs will become less involved in the movement and will not get worked efficiently.

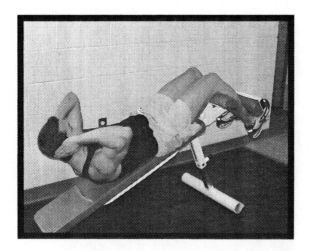

Decline Crunch

Hook your feet into the leg pads of the decline bench to stabilize your body and lie down. While lightly holding your hands behind your head, slowly raise yourself up until your reach about a 45 degree angle. Pause for a second and contract your abdominal muscles, then slowly lower your upper body until your back almost touches the pad. Right before your back is about to touch the pad, lift yourself up by contracting your abs.

Knee Raise

Place your elbows on the arm pads and grab hold of the handles with your hands. Let your feet dangle in the air using your upper arms to support your body. Now slowly lift your knees up until they are waist high, pause at the top, then lower your knees back to the starting position. To make the exercise more difficult, try to bring your hips off of the pad without using the momentum of your knees. This will allow you to give your lower abs a greater contraction.

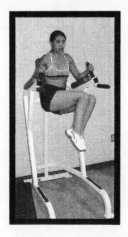

Tip: You can also vary the exercise by twisting your lower body and bringing your knees up so you can focus more on your oblique muscles.

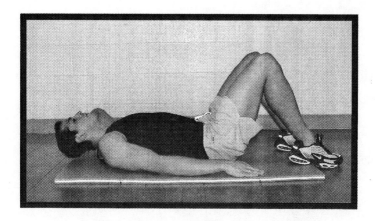

Side Crunch

Lie down on the floor with your knees bent and feet on the ground. Put one hand
on back of your head and leave the other on the floor. Begin lifting your shoulders
and torso off the floor and twist your upper body so that the elbow of your bent
hand is moving toward the knee of your opposite side. Pause at the top and
squeeze your oblique muscles (muscles on the side of your torso), then return
your torso to the floor in a slow controlled manner. Don't use your arm and jerk
your head to lift your torso off the floor.

Leg Exercises

Leg Press

Adjust the backrest to the lowest
setting and place your feet on the
platform. Your feet should be about
shoulder width apart and your back
firmly pressed against the back of
the seat. Extend your legs upward
and unlock the pegs that were
holding the weight up. Slowly lower
the weight until your legs form a
90 degree angle. Pause for a brief
second and then push the weight
up back to the starting position.
Don't lock out your legs at the end
of the movement for this will put
excess stress on your knee joints.
It is very important not to hold your
breath when pushing the weight up.
You should exhale when you extend
your legs and inhale when you lower
the weight.

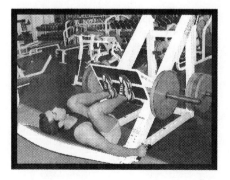

*Tip: Don't let your legs come down too far.
Your knees should not touch your chest and
your butt should not come off the pad.*

Barbell Squat

Step under the bar placing it on the upper part of your shoulders and slowly lift the weight off the rack. Take a few steps back and stand with your feet shoulder width apart and your body erect. Slowly lower your body downward by pushing your glutes (butt) backward and keeping your back straight. A good way to visualize this exercise is to pretend you are sitting in a chair. Lower your body until your legs are almost parallel to the ground and then push yourself upward towards the starting position. Try not to bend your body or your knees too much forward for this may increase your chances of injury. Make sure to keep your back as upright as possible. Although you will not be able to keep your back completely straight (there should be some bending forward in the movement), try to do the best you can.

Squats
(with or without dumbbells)

Stand with your body erect and you feet shoulder
width apart. You may want to stabilize your body
by holding on to something such as a chair or the
side of the wall. You can also hold a dumbbell in
both arms to add a bit more resistance to the
exercise. Slowly lower your body downward by
pushing your glutes (butt) backward until your
legs are almost parallel to the ground. Pause for
a brief second at the bottom and then push
yourself upward to the starting position. Try to
keep your back as upright as possible during the
exercise. Although you will not be able to keep
your back completely straight (there should be
some bending forward in the movement), do the
best you can.

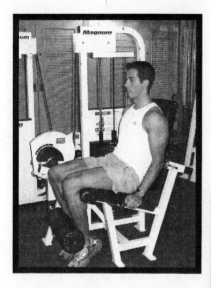

Leg Extension

Adjust the backrest so that when you sit on the machine, your back is straight and the back of your knees are touching the edge of the seat. Now adjust the roller pad so that it rests on the front of your ankles. Keeping your body erect with your body pressed firmly against the backrest, extend your legs and push the weight up. Pause at the top of the movement for a brief second, then slowly lower the weight back to the starting position. Make sure to exhale when pushing the weight up and inhaling when lowering the weight.

Tip: Do not raise or lower the weight only half way. This will reduce the effectiveness of the exercise.

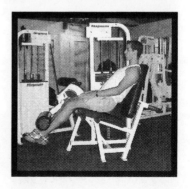

Tip: Don't adjust the seat too far back or let your butt come off the pad during the movement. If this happens, you are using too much weight.

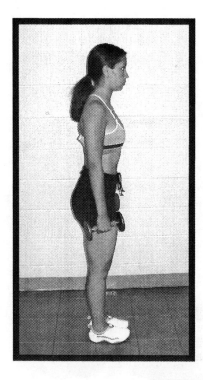

Tip: Your knee should form a 90 degree angle at the bottom of the movement and should not come over your feet when you step forward. Make sure to also go through the full range of motion and let your knee gently touch the ground.

Lunge With Dumbbells

Stand holding a pair of dumbbells in each hand and place them at your sides. Keeping your back straight, take a step forward with your left leg while keeping your right foot planted on the floor. When your foot hits the ground, do not move forward but rather lunge downward until your right knee barely touches the ground. Slowly push yourself up with your right leg and return to initial position. Complete a set and then repeat with the right leg.

Seated Hamstring Curl

Adjust the seat so that when you sit down, the backs of your knees are slightly hanging over the edge of the seat. Adjust the leg arm so that the pad touches the back of your ankles. Sit down on the machine and put your ankles on the leg arm. Push down the pad in front of you to lock in your legs. Now curl your legs downward until your legs forms a slightly greater then 90 degree angle. Pause for a second and slowly lower the weight back the starting position.

Leg Press
Calf Raise

Sit on a leg press machine with
your feet shoulder width apart
and the balls of your feet at the
edge of the platform. Straighten
out your legs until they are
almost locked out. Keeping your
knees stable, slowly lower your
heels until you feel a slight
stretch in the back of your legs,
then raise your heels as high as
you can. Pause at the top for a
second and then repeat.

*Tip: Don't change your foot position on this exercise. Your feet should stay facing forward at
all times. Changing your foot position will not work different parts of your calf.*

Seated Calf Raise

Sit in a calf-raise machine and position the balls of your feet at the edge of the platform. Lock your thighs underneath the kneepad, raise your heels, and unlock the bar. Begin the movement by slowly lowering your heels towards the floor until you feel a slight stretch in your calf muscles. When you feel a stretch, pause for a brief second and then raise your heels up by contracting your calf muscles. Raise your heels as high as you can, pause for a second at the top, and repeat.

Tip: Don't lean back and use your upper body to bring the weight up.

Stretches

Lower Back Stretch

Lie on your back, bring your knees up, and lock your hands together in back of your knees. Gently use your hands to pull both knees towards your chest, lifting your hips off the floor. You can vary the stretch by using one or both legs. Hold for 20 seconds and repeat.

Calf Stretch

Place the top of your foot on a platform or bottom of a bench and your heel on the floor. Now slowly lean forward till you feel a slight stretch in your calf. Hold for 20 seconds and repeat.

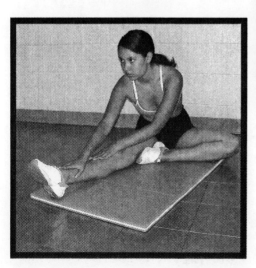

Hamstring Stretch

Lie down with one leg extended and one leg bent at the knee. Keeping your back straight, reach towards your toes until you feel a stretch in the back of your leg. Hold for 20 seconds and repeat with other side.

Chest, Shoulder, Bicep Stretch

Stand straight and extend your arm to hold onto a pole or side of a wall. Now rotate your torso away from your hand until you can feel a stretch in the front of your arm, shoulder, and chest. Do not lean away from the pole but rather let the turning of your upper body do the stretching. Hold for 20 seconds and repeat with other side.

Shoulder Stretch

Keeping your torso facing forward, grab your elbow and gently pull your arm across your body. You should feel a stretch in your shoulder and to a lesser extent the middle of your back. Hold for 20 seconds and repeat with other side.

Tricep Stretch

Sit on a bench and lift your arm over your head, bending your elbow as if you are trying to scratch your back. With the opposite arm, place your hand on back of your elbow and gently pull your arm backward and downward until you can feel a stretch in the back of your arm. Make sure not to pull down forcefully. A gently push is all that is needed to feel the stretch. Hold for 20 seconds and repeat with other side.

Inner Thigh Stretch

Sit erect on a the floor and bring the soles of your feet together. Now gently pull your heels towards your groin and press on the inside of your legs with your elbows so that your knees are moving towards the floor. Hold for 20 seconds and repeat with other side.

Quadriceps Stretch

Stand straight up and with your free hand, reach back and grasp the foot or ankle of your leg that is on the same side as your free hand. Bring your foot up to the ceiling until you can feel a stretch in the front of your leg. Be sure to keep your leg perpendicular to the floor and not bring the leg backward or forward. You may need to grasp a chair or something that you can support yourself with. Hold for 20 seconds and repeat with other side.

Back Stretch

Grab onto a bar or something that is waist-high and is an arm's length away. Bend your legs slightly and lower your upper body to the floor. Push your head through your arms until you feel a stretch in your upper back. Hold for 20 seconds and repeat.

Appendix C

Feeling Good for Life Training for Special Populations

It is likely that many people who want to use *Feeling Good for Life* also suffer from other medical conditions along with their depression. If you are over the age of 60 or struggle with arthritis, osteoporosis, hypertension, coronary heart disease, or diabetes, the guidelines in this section will help ensure that you have a safe and effective *Feeling Good for Life* Experience.

Exercise Guidelines for the Elderly

Before you begin any of the *Feeling Good for Life* Exercise Solutions, it is necessary for you to see your physician. As you know from filling out the *Feeling Good for Life* Readiness Questionnaire in chapter 2, men over the age of 40 and women over the age of 50 need to see a doctor before they start increasing their physical activity. Have your doctor review your medical history, perform a physical examination, and administer a treadmill test to see how physically fit you are. Based on this information, ask your doctor if she has any other guidelines than the ones presented below.

Your *Feeling Good for Life* Aerobic Solution should involve low-impact exercises such as cycling or the elliptical machine. You want to put as little stress as you can on your bones and joints so you don't increase your chances of any acute or chronic injury. The intensity of your program should be kept at the low end with your heart rate staying in the range of 30–60 percent of your maximum heart rate. Start out very slowly and gradually work your way up to your desired time with a max of 40 minutes.

During your *Feeling Good for Life* Weight Training Solution, perform high reps (between 8–15) with each rep being very slow and controlled (6–9 seconds per repetition). It is important that you go through the complete range of motion and do not perform partial reps just to lift heavier weight. Rest from 1–2 minutes between sets and wait at least 48 hours in between each workout session.

Adequate warm-up and cool-down periods are especially important since sudden cessation of exercise could cause excess stress on the heart. Your warm-up and cool-down should be 10–15 minutes performed at a low intensity. The long warm-up will prepare the body for movements required during your workout and the cool-down will gradually decrease your heart rate back to its normal state.

Conditions Associated with Old Age

Two major health problems that can accompany old age are arthritis and osteoporosis. These conditions can be incapacitating at times and can cause discomfort and distress if not properly treated. Although exercise improves both of these conditions, it is necessary to follow these guidelines because performing the wrong exercises or exercising to intensely could aggravate your existing problem. These recommendations will allow you to work within your capabilities and ensure you have a safe and effective workout.

Arthritis

Exercise is recommended for people with arthritis because it helps preserve muscle strength and joint mobility, relieves pain and stiffness, improves neuromuscular coordination, and prevents future problems associated with the condition. Your *Feeling Good for Life* Exercise Solution should be designed in conjunction with your doctor or physical therapist to make sure you are healthy enough to begin exercising.

Your *Feeling Good for Life* Aerobic Solution should include low impact activities, such as cycling, walking, or the elliptical machine and should be performed at a low intensity (40–70 percent of your maximum heart rate). The duration and intensity of the exercise should be reduced during periods of inflammation and pain. You will have to modify the intensity and duration of your workouts depending on how well you can handle the stress of exercise. If you are feeling pain after you exercise, take a day or two off and then resume at a lower intensity.

If you have severe arthritis, you may not be able to use some of the weight-bearing exercises in the *Feeling Good for Life* Weight Training Solution because they may cause you pain. If any exercise causes you pain, do not use it. You should use light resistance with higher reps (between 12–20) and perform all the movements the way they are described in appendix B. Poor posture and improper body alignment can disrupt performance as well decrease joint mobility and strength. It is vital that you put all your joints through their full range of motion at least once a day to maintain and improve mobility.

Osteoporosis

Individuals stricken with osteoporosis begin to experience a reduction in bone mass, which eventually increases the risk of fractures. Luckily, the *Feeling Good for Life* Exercise Solution will increase the strength of your bones and decrease many of the adverse effects of this condition. You will be able to use most of the *Feeling Good for Life* Exercise Solution programs outlined in chapters 2 and 3, but should follow these guidelines to decrease the chance of injury while exercising.

1) Avoid high impact aerobics such as jogging, running, or jumping.

2) Avoid hard surfaces that may become slippery when wet.

3) Do not pull on your neck while doing crunches.

4) Make sure to include weight training in your *Feeling Good for Life* Exercise Solution.

Coronary Heart Disease

Coronary heart disease (CHD) is the leading cause of death in the Western world and increases the risk of developing depression threefold. Moreover, people who are at risk for CHD and have depression increase their chances fourfold of suffering from a heart attack. Fortunately, exercise decreases the chances of developing both conditions.

Your *Feeling Good for Life* Aerobic Solution should consist of low intensity exercise, such as walking, stationary cycling, or low impact aerobics. Gradually increase the duration to 20–30 minutes of continuous movement with a heart rate ranging between 40–70 percent of your maximum heart rate. A longer warm-up and cool-down period of 10–15 minutes should be used to avoid increasing or decreasing your heart rate too rapidly.

During the *Feeling Good for Life* Weight Training Solution keep the resistance very low and perform 12–20 repetitions. Do not hold your breath during your workouts; this raises your blood pressure and works your heart more than necessary. Rest at least one minute between each set.

If you have recently suffered from any serious heart problems that required medical attention, it would be best to have graduated from a cardiac rehabilitation program as well as ask your physician if participation in one of the *Feeling Good for Life* Exercise Solutions is recommended. Make certain your physician provides you with an upper-limit heart rate so you will know when you are putting too much stress on your heart during exercise.

Hypertension

It has been estimated that as many as 50 million people in the United States have chronically elevated blood pressure (also called hypertension). Chronic hypertension can increase your risk of developing many other cardiovascular conditions, such as coronary heart disease (CHD) and stroke. Consistent exercise can decrease blood pressure by an average of 10 points.

Before starting your *Feeling Good for Life* Exercise Solution, it is necessary to get your doctor's permission. Your current medical status, the type(s) of medication you may be taking, and how well you have been managing your hypertension should be taken into consideration when designing your *Feeling Good for Life* Exercise Solution.

The frequency, duration, and intensity recommendations are basically the same as healthy individuals with a few special guidelines. First, it is extremely important that you do not hold your breath during weight training or moderate intensity aerobics. This can put extra stress on your heart by increasing your blood pressure. During your *Feeling Good for Life* Weight Training Solution, make a conscious effort to exhale upon exertion and inhale when bringing the weight down. Exercise should not continue if you notice any symptoms before, during, or immediately after exercise. If your symptoms persist, tell someone to contact emergency medical help. When the symptoms stop, contact your physician and do not resume exercise until your physician gives you clearance. Lastly, make sure to reevaluate your *Feeling Good for Life* Exercise Solution whenever your physician gives you new medication. Your physician may have to modify your program based on the side effects of the medication.

Diabetes

Diabetes is characterized by a reduction in the secretion of insulin by the pancreas or decreased sensitivity to insulin itself. The result is abnormalities in the metabolism of carbohydrates, protein, and fat. If left untreated, other health problems such as kidney failure, nerve disorders, eye problems, and heart disease can arise. Research has shown that diabetics also have a three to four times greater risk of developing depression. Exercise counteracts these problems by improving insulin receptor sensitivity and increasing the number of receptors for insulin. By exercising regularly you can reduce your symptoms of diabetes, possibly to the point where you will no longer need to take medication.

The exercise guidelines for diabetics are similar to those outlined in chapters 2 and 3. The additional recommendations here are necessary for you to follow regardless of which *Feeling Good for Life* Exercise Solution you use. If you do not follow these recommendations, you may be putting yourself at risk for injury and an episode involving symptoms of diabetes.

1) Try not to exercise during periods when insulin is active or you just recently used insulin medication. During this time your blood sugar levels will be low and interfere with exercise.

2) Do not inject insulin into any of the muscle groups that you will be using during your exercise session, because it may be absorbed too quickly resulting in hypoglycemia.

3) Always carry a quick absorbing carbohydrate source, such as juice or candy, in case hypoglycemia occurs.

4) If you are going to exercise for a prolonged period of time, you should snack on something with carbohydrates before and during exercise.

5) Check your blood sugar level consistently.

6) Try to exercise at the same time each day to better control your blood sugar levels.

Appendix D

Feeling Good for Life Journal

Week #1

Name _____

Weekly Goals_____

_____

Reward if You Accomplish Weekly Goals_____

_____

Date_____

Type of Exercise Performed_____ Duration_____

How Do You Feel Today—*(Depressed) 1 2 3 4 5 6 7 8 9 10 (Great)*

Comments _____

_____

_____

_____

_____

_____

_____

Date_____

Type of Exercise Performed_____ Duration_____

How Do You Feel Today—*(Depressed) 1 2 3 4 5 6 7 8 9 10 (Great)*

Comments

_____
_____
_____
_____
_____
_____
_____
_____

Date_____

Type of Exercise Performed_____ Duration_____

How Do You Feel Today—*(Depressed) 1 2 3 4 5 6 7 8 9 10 (Great)*

Comments _____

_____
_____
_____
_____
_____
_____
_____

Date_____

Type of Exercise Performed_____ Duration_____

How Do You Feel Today—*(Depressed) 1 2 3 4 5 6 7 8 9 10 (Great)*

Comments _____
_____
_____
_____
_____
_____
_____

Date_____

Type of Exercise Performed_____ Duration_____

How Do You Feel Today—*(Depressed) 1 2 3 4 5 6 7 8 9 10 (Great)*

Comments _____
_____
_____
_____
_____
_____
_____

Date_____

Type of Exercise Performed_____ Duration_____

How Do You Feel Today—*(Depressed) 1 2 3 4 5 6 7 8 9 10 (Great)*

Comments _____
_____
_____
_____
_____
_____
_____

Date_____

Type of Exercise Performed_____ Duration_____

How Do You Feel Today—*(Depressed) 1 2 3 4 5 6 7 8 9 10 (Great)*

Comments _____
_____
_____
_____
_____
_____
_____

How Did I Feel This Week? *Depressed — Bad — Fair — Good — Great*
Comments_____

_____
_____
_____
_____
_____
_____
_____
_____
_____
_____
_____

Week #2

Name _____

Weekly Goals_____
_____

Reward if You Accomplish Weekly Goals_____
_____

Date_____

Type of Exercise Performed_____ Duration_____

How Do You Feel Today—*(Depressed) 1 2 3 4 5 6 7 8 9 10 (Great)*

Comments _____
_____
_____
_____
_____
_____
_____
_____

Date_____

Type of Exercise Performed_____ Duration_____

How Do You Feel Today—*(Depressed) 1 2 3 4 5 6 7 8 9 10 (Great)*

Comments

_____

_____

_____

_____

_____

_____

_____

Date_____

Type of Exercise Performed_____ Duration_____

How Do You Feel Today—*(Depressed) 1 2 3 4 5 6 7 8 9 10 (Great)*

Comments _____

_____

_____

_____

_____

_____

_____

_____

Date_____

Type of Exercise Performed_____ Duration_____

How Do You Feel Today—*(Depressed) 1 2 3 4 5 6 7 8 9 10 (Great)*

Comments _____

_____

_____

_____

_____

_____

_____

_____

Date_____

Type of Exercise Performed_____ Duration_____

How Do You Feel Today—*(Depressed) 1 2 3 4 5 6 7 8 9 10 (Great)*

Comments _____

_____

_____

_____

_____

_____

_____

Date_____

Type of Exercise Performed_____ Duration_____

How Do You Feel Today—*(Depressed) 1 2 3 4 5 6 7 8 9 10 (Great)*

Comments _____
_____
_____
_____
_____
_____
_____

Date_____

Type of Exercise Performed_____ Duration_____

How Do You Feel Today—*(Depressed) 1 2 3 4 5 6 7 8 9 10 (Great)*

Comments _____
_____
_____
_____
_____
_____
_____

How Did I Feel This Week? *Depressed — Bad — Fair — Good — Great*
Comments_____

_____

_____

_____

_____

_____

_____

_____

_____

_____

Week #3

Name _____

Weekly Goals_____
_____

Reward if You Accomplish Weekly Goals_____
_____

Date_____

Type of Exercise Performed_____ Duration_____

How Do You Feel Today—*(Depressed) 1 2 3 4 5 6 7 8 9 10 (Great)*

Comments _____
_____
_____
_____
_____
_____
_____

Date_____

Type of Exercise Performed_____ Duration_____

How Do You Feel Today—*(Depressed) 1 2 3 4 5 6 7 8 9 10 (Great)*

Comments

_____

_____

_____

_____

_____

_____

_____

_____

Date_____

Type of Exercise Performed_____ Duration_____

How Do You Feel Today—*(Depressed) 1 2 3 4 5 6 7 8 9 10 (Great)*

Comments _____

_____

_____

_____

_____

_____

_____

_____

Date_____

Type of Exercise Performed_____ Duration_____

How Do You Feel Today—*(Depressed) 1 2 3 4 5 6 7 8 9 10 (Great)*

Comments _____
_____
_____
_____
_____
_____
_____

Date_____

Type of Exercise Performed_____ Duration_____

How Do You Feel Today—*(Depressed) 1 2 3 4 5 6 7 8 9 10 (Great)*

Comments _____
_____
_____
_____
_____
_____
_____

Date_____

Type of Exercise Performed_____ Duration_____

How Do You Feel Today—*(Depressed)* *1 2 3 4 5 6 7 8 9 10 (Great)*

Comments _____

_____

_____

_____

_____

_____

_____

_____

Date_____

Type of Exercise Performed_____ Duration_____

How Do You Feel Today—*(Depressed)* *1 2 3 4 5 6 7 8 9 10 (Great)*

Comments _____

_____

_____

_____

_____

_____

_____

_____

How Did I Feel This Week? *Depressed — Bad — Fair — Good — Great*
Comments_____

_____

_____

_____

_____

_____

_____

_____

_____

_____

_____

Week #4

Name _____

Weekly Goals_____

_____

Reward if You Accomplish Weekly Goals_____

_____

Date_____

Type of Exercise Performed_____ Duration_____

How Do You Feel Today—*(Depressed) 1 2 3 4 5 6 7 8 9 10 (Great)*

Comments _____

_____

_____

_____

_____

_____

_____

Date_____

Type of Exercise Performed_____ Duration_____

How Do You Feel Today—*(Depressed) 1 2 3 4 5 6 7 8 9 10 (Great)*

Comments

_____

_____

_____

_____

_____

_____

_____

_____

Date_____

Type of Exercise Performed_____ Duration_____

How Do You Feel Today—*(Depressed) 1 2 3 4 5 6 7 8 9 10 (Great)*

Comments _____

_____

_____

_____

_____

_____

_____

_____

Date_____

Type of Exercise Performed_____ Duration_____

How Do You Feel Today—*(Depressed) 1 2 3 4 5 6 7 8 9 10 (Great)*

Comments _____
_____
_____
_____
_____
_____
_____
_____

Date_____

Type of Exercise Performed_____ Duration_____

How Do You Feel Today—*(Depressed) 1 2 3 4 5 6 7 8 9 10 (Great)*

Comments _____
_____
_____
_____
_____
_____
_____
_____

Date_____

Type of Exercise Performed_____ **Duration**_____

How Do You Feel Today—*(Depressed) 1 2 3 4 5 6 7 8 9 10 (Great)*

Comments _____

_____

_____

_____

_____

_____

_____

Date_____

Type of Exercise Performed_____ **Duration**_____

How Do You Feel Today—*(Depressed) 1 2 3 4 5 6 7 8 9 10 (Great)*

Comments _____

_____

_____

_____

_____

_____

_____

How Did I Feel This Week? *Depressed — Bad — Fair — Good — Great*
Comments_____
_____
_____
_____
_____
_____
_____
_____
_____
_____
_____

Week #5

Name _____

Weekly Goals_____
_____

Reward if You Accomplish Weekly Goals_____
_____

Date_____

Type of Exercise Performed_____ Duration_____

How Do You Feel Today—*(Depressed) 1 2 3 4 5 6 7 8 9 10 (Great)*

Comments _____
_____
_____
_____
_____
_____
_____

Date_____

Type of Exercise Performed_____ Duration_____

How Do You Feel Today—*(Depressed) 1 2 3 4 5 6 7 8 9 10 (Great)*

Comments

_____

_____

_____

_____

_____

_____

_____

_____

Date_____

Type of Exercise Performed_____ Duration_____

How Do You Feel Today—*(Depressed) 1 2 3 4 5 6 7 8 9 10 (Great)*

Comments _____

_____

_____

_____

_____

_____

_____

_____

Date_____

Type of Exercise Performed_____ Duration_____

How Do You Feel Today—*(Depressed) 1 2 3 4 5 6 7 8 9 10 (Great)*

Comments _____

_____

_____

_____

_____

_____

_____

Date_____

Type of Exercise Performed_____ Duration_____

How Do You Feel Today—*(Depressed) 1 2 3 4 5 6 7 8 9 10 (Great)*

Comments _____

_____

_____

_____

_____

_____

_____

Date_____

Type of Exercise Performed_____ Duration_____

How Do You Feel Today—*(Depressed) 1 2 3 4 5 6 7 8 9 10 (Great)*

Comments _____
_____
_____
_____
_____
_____
_____

Date_____

Type of Exercise Performed_____ Duration_____

How Do You Feel Today—*(Depressed) 1 2 3 4 5 6 7 8 9 10 (Great)*

Comments _____
_____
_____
_____
_____
_____
_____

How Did I Feel This Week? *Depressed — Bad — Fair — Good — Great*
Comments_____

_____

_____

_____

_____

_____

_____

_____

_____

_____

_____

Week #6

Name _____

Weekly Goals_____

_____

Reward if You Accomplish Weekly Goals_____

_____

Date_____

Type of Exercise Performed_____ Duration_____

How Do You Feel Today—*(Depressed) 1 2 3 4 5 6 7 8 9 10 (Great)*

Comments _____

_____

_____

_____

_____

_____

_____

Date_____

Type of Exercise Performed_____ Duration_____

How Do You Feel Today—*(Depressed) 1 2 3 4 5 6 7 8 9 10 (Great)*

Comments

_____

_____

_____

_____

_____

_____

_____

_____

Date_____

Type of Exercise Performed_____ Duration_____

How Do You Feel Today—*(Depressed) 1 2 3 4 5 6 7 8 9 10 (Great)*

Comments _____

_____

_____

_____

_____

_____

_____

Date_____

Type of Exercise Performed_____ Duration_____

How Do You Feel Today—*(Depressed) 1 2 3 4 5 6 7 8 9 10 (Great)*

Comments _____
_____
_____
_____
_____
_____
_____
_____

Date_____

Type of Exercise Performed_____ Duration_____

How Do You Feel Today—*(Depressed) 1 2 3 4 5 6 7 8 9 10 (Great)*

Comments _____
_____
_____
_____
_____
_____
_____

Date_____

Type of Exercise Performed_____ Duration_____

How Do You Feel Today—*(Depressed) 1 2 3 4 5 6 7 8 9 10 (Great)*

Comments _____
_____
_____
_____
_____
_____
_____

Date_____

Type of Exercise Performed_____ Duration_____

How Do You Feel Today—*(Depressed) 1 2 3 4 5 6 7 8 9 10 (Great)*

Comments _____
_____
_____
_____
_____
_____
_____

How Did I Feel This Week? *Depressed — Bad — Fair — Good — Great*
Comments_____

_____

_____

_____

_____

_____

_____

_____

_____

_____

_____

_____

Week #7

Name _____

Weekly Goals_____

_____

Reward if You Accomplish Weekly Goals_____

_____

Date_____

Type of Exercise Performed_____ Duration_____

How Do You Feel Today—*(Depressed) 1 2 3 4 5 6 7 8 9 10 (Great)*

Comments _____

_____

_____

_____

_____

_____

_____

_____

Date_____

Type of Exercise Performed_____ **Duration**_____

How Do You Feel Today—*(Depressed) 1 2 3 4 5 6 7 8 9 10 (Great)*

Comments

_____
_____
_____
_____
_____
_____
_____
_____

Date_____

Type of Exercise Performed_____ **Duration**_____

How Do You Feel Today—*(Depressed) 1 2 3 4 5 6 7 8 9 10 (Great)*

Comments _____

_____
_____
_____
_____
_____
_____
_____

Date_____

Type of Exercise Performed_____ Duration_____

How Do You Feel Today—*(Depressed)* *1 2 3 4 5 6 7 8 9 10* *(Great)*

Comments _____

_____

_____

_____

_____

_____

_____

_____

Date_____

Type of Exercise Performed_____ Duration_____

How Do You Feel Today—*(Depressed)* *1 2 3 4 5 6 7 8 9 10* *(Great)*

Comments _____

_____

_____

_____

_____

_____

_____

_____

Date_____

Type of Exercise Performed_____ Duration_____

How Do You Feel Today—*(Depressed)* *1 2 3 4 5 6 7 8 9 10* *(Great)*

Comments _____

_____

_____

_____

_____

_____

_____

_____

Date_____

Type of Exercise Performed_____ Duration_____

How Do You Feel Today—*(Depressed)* *1 2 3 4 5 6 7 8 9 10* *(Great)*

Comments _____

_____

_____

_____

_____

_____

_____

How Did I Feel This Week? *Depressed — Bad — Fair — Good — Great*
Comments_____

_____

_____

_____

_____

_____

_____

_____

_____

_____

_____

Week #8

Name _____

Weekly Goals_____

_____

Reward if You Accomplish Weekly Goals_____

_____

Date_____

Type of Exercise Performed_____ Duration_____

How Do You Feel Today—*(Depressed) 1 2 3 4 5 6 7 8 9 10 (Great)*

Comments _____

_____

_____

_____

_____

_____

_____

_____

Date_____

Type of Exercise Performed_____ **Duration**_____

How Do You Feel Today—*(Depressed)* *1 2 3 4 5 6 7 8 9 10 (Great)*

Comments

_____
_____
_____
_____
_____
_____
_____
_____

Date_____

Type of Exercise Performed_____ **Duration**_____

How Do You Feel Today—*(Depressed)* *1 2 3 4 5 6 7 8 9 10 (Great)*

Comments _____

_____
_____
_____
_____
_____
_____
_____

Date_____

Type of Exercise Performed_____ Duration_____

How Do You Feel Today—*(Depressed) 1 2 3 4 5 6 7 8 9 10 (Great)*

Comments _____
_____
_____
_____
_____
_____
_____
_____

Date_____

Type of Exercise Performed_____ Duration_____

How Do You Feel Today—*(Depressed) 1 2 3 4 5 6 7 8 9 10 (Great)*

Comments _____
_____
_____
_____
_____
_____
_____
_____

Date_____

Type of Exercise Performed_____ Duration_____

How Do You Feel Today—*(Depressed) 1 2 3 4 5 6 7 8 9 10 (Great)*

Comments _____
_____
_____
_____
_____
_____
_____
_____

Date_____

Type of Exercise Performed_____ Duration_____

How Do You Feel Today—*(Depressed) 1 2 3 4 5 6 7 8 9 10 (Great)*

Comments _____
_____
_____
_____
_____
_____
_____

How Did I Feel This Week? *Depressed — Bad — Fair — Good — Great*
Comments_____

_____

_____

_____

_____

_____

_____

_____

_____

_____

_____

Week #9

Name _____

Weekly Goals_____

_____

Reward if You Accomplish Weekly Goals_____

_____

Date_____

Type of Exercise Performed_____ Duration_____

How Do You Feel Today—*(Depressed) 1 2 3 4 5 6 7 8 9 10 (Great)*

Comments _____

_____

_____

_____

_____

_____

_____

_____

Date_____

Type of Exercise Performed_____ Duration_____

How Do You Feel Today—*(Depressed) 1 2 3 4 5 6 7 8 9 10 (Great)*

Comments

_____

_____

_____

_____

_____

_____

_____

_____

Date_____

Type of Exercise Performed_____ Duration_____

How Do You Feel Today—*(Depressed) 1 2 3 4 5 6 7 8 9 10 (Great)*

Comments _____

_____

_____

_____

_____

_____

_____

_____

Date_____

Type of Exercise Performed_____ Duration_____

How Do You Feel Today—*(Depressed)* *1 2 3 4 5 6 7 8 9 10* *(Great)*

Comments _____
_____
_____
_____
_____
_____
_____
_____

Date_____

Type of Exercise Performed_____ Duration_____

How Do You Feel Today—*(Depressed)* *1 2 3 4 5 6 7 8 9 10* *(Great)*

Comments _____
_____
_____
_____
_____
_____
_____

Date_____

Type of Exercise Performed_____ Duration_____

How Do You Feel Today—*(Depressed) 1 2 3 4 5 6 7 8 9 10 (Great)*

Comments _____
_____
_____
_____
_____
_____
_____
_____

Date_____

Type of Exercise Performed_____ Duration_____

How Do You Feel Today—*(Depressed) 1 2 3 4 5 6 7 8 9 10 (Great)*

Comments _____
_____
_____
_____
_____
_____
_____

How Did I Feel This Week? *Depressed — Bad — Fair — Good — Great*
Comments_____

_____

_____

_____

_____

_____

_____

_____

_____

_____

_____

Week #10

Name _____

Weekly Goals_____
_____

Reward if You Accomplish Weekly Goals_____
_____

Date_____

Type of Exercise Performed_____ Duration_____

How Do You Feel Today—*(Depressed) 1 2 3 4 5 6 7 8 9 10 (Great)*

Comments _____
_____
_____
_____
_____
_____
_____
_____

Date_____

Type of Exercise Performed_____ Duration_____

How Do You Feel Today—*(Depressed) 1 2 3 4 5 6 7 8 9 10 (Great)*

Comments

_____
_____
_____
_____
_____
_____
_____

Date_____

Type of Exercise Performed_____ Duration_____

How Do You Feel Today—*(Depressed) 1 2 3 4 5 6 7 8 9 10 (Great)*

Comments _____

_____
_____
_____
_____
_____
_____
_____

Date_____

Type of Exercise Performed_____ Duration_____

How Do You Feel Today—*(Depressed) 1 2 3 4 5 6 7 8 9 10 (Great)*

Comments _____
_____
_____
_____
_____
_____
_____
_____

Date_____

Type of Exercise Performed_____ Duration_____

How Do You Feel Today—*(Depressed) 1 2 3 4 5 6 7 8 9 10 (Great)*

Comments _____
_____
_____
_____
_____
_____
_____

Date_____

Type of Exercise Performed_____ Duration_____

How Do You Feel Today—*(Depressed) 1 2 3 4 5 6 7 8 9 10 (Great)*

Comments _____
_____
_____
_____
_____
_____
_____

Date_____

Type of Exercise Performed_____ Duration_____

How Do You Feel Today—*(Depressed) 1 2 3 4 5 6 7 8 9 10 (Great)*

Comments _____
_____
_____
_____
_____
_____
_____

How Did I Feel This Week? *Depressed — Bad — Fair — Good — Great*
Comments_____

_____
_____
_____
_____
_____
_____
_____
_____
_____
_____

Appendix E

Feeling Good for Life Progress Sheets

The *Feeling Good for Life* Muscle Building Solution

Date_____   Workout #2: Lower Body

Muscle Group	Exercise	Sets	Reps	Weight	Actual Reps
Chest	1)	1	12–15		
	2)	1	10–12		
	3)	1	8–10		
Back	1)	1	12–15		
	2)	1	10–12		
	3)	1	8–10		
Bicep	1)	1	12–15		
	2)	1	10–12		
	3)	1	8–10		
Triceps	1)	1	12–15		
	2)	1	10–12		
	3)	1	8–10		

Date_____   Workout #2: Lower Body

Muscle Group	Exercise	Sets	Reps	Weight	Actual Reps
Quads/Glutes	1)	1	15		
	2)	1	12–15		
	3)	1	10–12		
Hamstring	1)	1	15		
	2)	1	12–15		
		1	10–12		
Shoulders	1)	1	12–15		
	2)	1	10–12		
	3)	1	8–10		
Calves	1)	1	15		
	2)	1	12–15		
		1	10–12		
Abs	1)	1	15		
	2)	1	12–15		
		1	10–12		

Feeling Good for Life Circuit Solution

Date_____

Muscle Group	Exercise	Circuits	Reps	Weight	Actual Reps
Quads/Glutes		3	12–15		
Hamstrings		3	12–15		
Back		3	12–15		
Chest		3	12–15		
Shoulders		3	12–15		
Trapezius		3	12–15		
Triceps		3	12–15		
Biceps		3	12–15		
Calves		3	12–15		
Abs		3	12–15		
Lower Back		3	12–15		

Appendix F

Getting Personal–How to
Choose the Right Personal Trainer

Having your very own personal trainer can provide you with that extra edge in getting in shape and becoming depression free. A personal trainer can help with your motivation because you will have an expert in field of health and fitness giving you personalized attention to help you meet your mental and physical health goals. However, personal trainers vary greatly, not only in educational background and costs, but also in their training and nutritional philosophy. So you should make sure that you get a personal trainer that fits well and will help you achieve your goals.

The first place to look for a trainer is a health club near your home or workplace. Most gyms have at least one certified trainer. If they don't, they will point you to a place that has one. You can also look into hiring a personal trainer who owns his or her own studio. These places can have low membership, providing you with a quiet, personal atmosphere unlike a busy club. You can also ask friends for recommendations.

Once you have narrowed down a list of several personal trainers, set up interviews. It is essential for you to find a personal trainer you have a connection with. You are going to be spending 2–3 one-hour session per week with this person, so you better make sure that this time will be enjoyable.

When you call or meet with the personal trainers, you should ask them the following questions:

1) What level of education and certification do you have and how much practical experience do you have?

   a. Thousands of individuals call themselves personal trainers even though they are not properly certified. Look for trainers that are certified by an accredited professional organization such as ACE (American Council on Exercise), National Strength and Condition Association (NSCA), or American College of Sports Medicine (ACSM).

2) Ask for client references.

   a. If your trainer does not have satisfied customers, who is to say that you will be satisfied? The trainer should be able to give you the names of two or three of their clients so you can call and ask what type of trainer they are. If they are not willing to give you references, then you should look for another trainer.

3) Does the trainer or the gym have insurance?

4) Ask for proof of current certification in CPR.

   a. Required for most certified personal trainers.

5) Make sure your schedules match up.

   a. Find a trainer that can meet at times convenient for you.

6) What are the rates?

    a. This answer can very greatly from trainer to trainer. Some will cost $20 per hour while others can cost $100 per hour.

7) What is the facility like where the trainer works?

    a. Make sure that the gym is close to work or home and that it is clean and well kept.

8) What type of training will I be doing with you?

After you have met with the trainer, you now have to ask yourself a number of questions. Did the trainer seem professional, pleasant, and motivating? Did the trainer seem to have good listening and communication skills? More importantly, will you get along with this trainer and look forward to working with him or her?

Appendix G

Choosing the Right Gym

Along with other major investments in your life such as moving to a new city, buying a home, or deciding to take a new job, joining a health club is a serious investment of your time and money. If you join a gym that is not suited to your lifestyle, then you will be more likely to skip your workouts, resulting in lost money and weakened chances to begin *Feeling Good for Life*. This is why it is necessary to do some research before you sign up for a gym membership.

The first thing you want to consider is how convenient the gym is to where you live or work. Studies have shown that people who live or work close to their gym work out more often. You don't want to be spending a chunk of your time getting to and from the gym, so look for one that is easily accessible.

Next, take inventory while at the health club. Make a list of what is important to you in a gym and take that list with you. Do they have the type of equipment you need (plenty of free weights and machines)? Do they offer a number of group exercise classes you would be interested in taking? Do they have childcare? Write down these requirements and check them off when you visit the gym.

Next, set an appointment to speak with a sales representative and get a tour of the facility. Make sure to leave your credit card and checkbook at home. The sales rep will most likely try to pressure you into buying a membership that "ends that day" or will try to get you to sign a long-term contract. What you want to emphasize is that you are just looking for now. It is necessary that you learn everything you can about the club so you can make an informed decision about joining.

While you are at the facility, take the time to look over the equipment. Is it clean? Do the machines look old? Are the free weights all over the gym? Go into the bathrooms and locker rooms and see if everything is clean. Check the general atmosphere of the gym. Is it noisy and too full? Is there adequate ventilation?

Pay special attention to the staff. Do they seem to have a good attitude? Are they polite and helpful or do they all seem to be in a rush? Do they have personal trainers? How much extra are training sessions? Also, talk to members and see if they are satisfied with the club.

Many health clubs offer free week-long passes, so before you sign up try the gym for a week to see if you like it. Go at peak and off-peak hours to see what the atmosphere is like at times you will be going to the gym. Trying the gym out will enable you to use the equipment and get a general feel for the place before you make the commitment to sign up for a membership.

When you have found the gym you are interested in, always read the contract front and back. Too many sales representatives sell packages without going into enough detail about what the contract entails. The end result is you signing up for something that you did not want. Many times they will lock you into a year or two-year contract without you realizing it. Make sure to find out about the termination policies. If necessary, take the contract home with you so you can read it.

Appendix H

Resources

Depression

The organizations below can provide you with useful information and services for people with depression.

Agency for Health Care Policy and Research (AHCPR)
AHCPR Publications Clearinghouse
P.O. Box 8547
Silver Spring, MD 20907-8547
Phone: (800) 358-9295
Website: www.ahcpr.gov
E-mail: info@ahcpr.gov

American Psychiatric Association
1400 K Street, NW
Washington D.C. 20005
Phone: (202) 682-6220
Website: www.psych.org
E-mail: apa@psych.org

American Psychological Association
750 First Street, NE
Washington D.C. 20002-4242
Phone: (202) 336-5500
Website: www.apa.org

Depression Alliance
http://www.depressionalliance.org/

Depression and Related Affective Disorders Association (DRADA)
Neyer 3-181, 600 N. Wolfe Street
Baltimore, MD 21287-7381
Phone: (410) 955-4647
Website: www.hopkinsmedicine.org/drada
E-mail: drada@jhmi.edu

Dr. Ivan Goldberg's Depression Central
Created by: Ivan Goldberg, MD
Suite 407
1556 Third Avenue
New York, NY 10128
Phone: (212) 876 7800
Website: http://www.psycom.net/depression.central.html

National Alliance for the Mentally Ill
200 N. Glebe Road, suite 1015
Arlington, VA 22203-3754
Phone: (800) 950-6264
Website: www.nami.org

National Depressive and Manic Depressive Association
730 Franklin, suite 501
Chicago, IL 60610-3526
Phone: (800) 826-3632
Website: www.ndmda.org
Email: myrtis@aol.com

National Foundation for Depressive Illness
P.O. Box 2257
New York, NY 10116
Phone: (800) 239-1265
Website: www.depression.org

National Institute of Mental Health
Public Inquiries Office
5600 Fisher Lane, room 7c-02, MSC 8030
Bethesda, MD 20892-8030
Phone: (301) 443-4513
Website: www.nimh.gov
E-mail: nimhinfo@nih.gov

National Mental Health Association
1021 Prince Street
Alexandria, VA 22314-2971
Phone: (800) 969-6642
Website: www.nmha.org

Exercise

American College of Sports Medicine
Phone: (801) 212-3472
Website: www.acsm.org
E-mail: ioc.worldcongress@saltlake2002.com

American Council on Exercise
5820 Oberlin Drive, Suite 102
San Diego, CA 92121-3787
Phone: (858) 535-8227
Website: www.acefitness.org

National Strength and Conditioning Association
955 N. Union Blvd.
Colorado Springs, CO 80909
Phone: (719) 632-6722
Website: http://www.nsca-lift.org/
E-mail: commission@nsca-cc.org

References

Chapter 1

American Medical Association. 1998. *Essential Guide to Depression.* New York: Pocket Books.

American Psychiatric Association. 1994. *Diagnostic and Statistical Manual of Mental Disorders: 4th Edition.* Washington, D.C. American Psychiatric Association.

Bailey, S.P., Davis, J.M., & Ahlborn, E.N. 1993. Serotonergic agonists and antagonists affect endurance performance in the rat. *International Journal Sports Medicine 14(6): 330-33.*

Blair, S.N., Kannel, W.B., Kohl, H.W., Goodyear, N., & Wilson, P.W.F. 1989. Surrogate measures of physical activity and physical fitness: evidence for sedentary treatment of resting tachycardia, obesity and low vital capacity. *American Journal of Epidemiology 129:* 1145-56.

Byrne, A. & Byrne, D.G. 1993. The effects of exercise on depression, anxiety and other mood states: a review. *Journal of Psychosomatic Research* *37(6)*: 565-74.

Carlson, N.R. 1999. *Foundations of Physiological Psychology*. Needham, MA: Allyn and Bacon.

Chaouloff, F. 1989. About the effect of L-tryptophan on exercise performance. *International Journal of Medicine 10*: 383.

Chaouloff, F., Elghozi, J.L., Guezunnec, Y., & Laude, D.1985. Effects of conditioned running on Plasma liver and brain tryptophan on the brain 5-hydroxyytryptamine metabolism of the rat. *British Journal of Pharmacology 86*: 33-41.

Chaouloff F., Kennett, G.A., Serrurier, B., Merino, D., & Curzon, G.1986. Amino acid analysis demonstrates that increased plasma free tryptophan causes the increase of brain tryptophan during exercise in the rat. *Journal of Neurochemistry 6*: 1647-50.

Chaouloff F., Laude, D., & Elghozi, J.L. 1989. Physical exercise: Evidence for differential consequences of tryptophan on 5-HT synthesis and metabolism in central Serotonergic cell bodies and terminals. *Journal of Neural Transmission 78*: 121-130.

Chaouloff F., Laude, D., Guezennec, Y., & Elghozi, J.L. 1986. Motor activity increases tryptophan 5-hydroxyindoleacetic acid, and homovanillic acid in ventricular cerebrospinal fluid of the conscious rat. *Journal of Neurochemistry 46*: 1313-16.

Chaouloff F., Laude, D., Merino, D., Serru-methyl-p-tyrosine affect the exercise-induced imbalance between the availability of tryptophan and synthesis of serotonin in the brain of the rat. *Neuropharmocology 26:* 1099-1106.

Chaouloff F., Laude, D., Merino, D., Serrurier, B., Guezennec, Y., & Elghozi, J.L. 1987. Brain serotonin response to exercise in the rat: The influence of training duration. *Biogenic Amines 4:* 99-106.

Cooper, J.R., Bloom, F.E., & Roth, R.*H.* 1986. *The Biochemical Basis of Neuropharmocology (5th ed.).* New York: Oxford University Press.

Craft, L.L., Landers, L.M. 1998. The effect on clinical Depression and depression resulting from Mental Illness: A meta-Analysis. *Journal of Sport and Exercise Psychology 20,* 339-57.

Delgado, P.L., Charney, D.S., Price, L.H., Aghajanian, G.K., Landis, H., & Hininger G.R. 1990. Serotonin Function and the Mechanism of Antidepressant Action. *Archives of General Psychiatry 47:* 411-18.

De Meirleir, K., et al. 1986. Beta-endorphin and ACTH levels in peripheral blood during and after aerobic and anaerobic exercise. *European Journal of Applied Physiology 55:* 5-8.

Dishman, R.K. 1996. Brain monoamines, exercise and behavioral stress: animal models. *Medicine and Science in Sports and Exercise 29:* 63-74.

Dishman, R.K., Renner, S.D., & Youngstedt, et al. 1997. Active wheel running reduces escape latency and alters brain monoamine levels after foot shock. *Brain Research Bulletin 43(5):* 399-406.

Donevan, R.H. & Andrew, G.M. 1987. Plasma-endorphin immunore-activity during graded cycle ergometry. *Medicine and Science in Sports and Exercise 19*: 229-33.

Estrada, E.D., et al. 1996. Stimulation of glucose uptake by the natural coenzyme alpha lipoic acid/thioctic acid: participation of elements of insulin signaling pathway. *Diabetes 45*: 1798-1804.

Fescher, H.G., Hollmann, W., & De Meirleir, K. 1991. Exercise changes in plasma tryptophan fractions and relationship with prolactin. *International Journal of Sports Medicine 12*: 487-89.

Fletcher, G.F., Blair, S.N., et al. 1992. Statement on exercise: Benefits and recommendations for physical activity programs for all Americas. *Circulation 86:* 340-44.

Franz, S.I., & Hamilton, G.V. 1905. The effects of exercise upon retardation in conditions of depression. *American Journal of Insanity 762:* 239-56.

Gavard, J.A., Lustman, P.J., & Cloise, R.E 1993. Prevalence of depression in adults with diabetes: An epidemiological evaluation. *Diabetes Care 16:* 1167-78.

Gerin, C., Becquet, D., & Private, A. 1995. Direct evidence for the link between monoaminergic pathways and motor activity. I. A study with microdyalysis probes implanted in the ventral funiculis of the spinal cord. *Brain Research 704:* 191-201.

Gern, C., Legrand, A., & Privat, A. 1994. Study of 5-HT release in chronically implanted microdyalysis probe in the ventral horn of the spinal cord of unrestrained rats during exercise on a treadmill. *Journal of Neuroscience 53.* 129-41.

Goldfarb, A.H., Hatfield, B.D., Armstrong, D., & Potts, J. 1990. Plasma beta-endorphin concentration: Response to intensity and duration of exercise. *Medicine and Science in Sports and Exercise 22:* 241-44.

Goldfarb, A.H., Hatfield, B.D., Potts, J., & Armstrong, D. 1991. Beta-endorphin time course response to intensity of exercise: Effect of training status. *International Journal of Sports and Medicine 12:* 435-48.

Hatfield, B.D., et al. 1987. Serum beta-endorphin and affective response to graded exercise in young and elderly men. *Journal of Gerontology 42:* 429-431.

Jacob, S., Streeper, R.S., et al. 1995. The antioxidant alpha lipoic acid enhances insulin stimulated glucose metabolism in insulin-resistant skeletal muscle. *Diabetes 45:* 1024-29.

Khamaisi, M., Potashnik, R., et al. 1997. Lipoic acid reduces glycemia and increases muscle GLUT4 content in streptozotocin-diabetic mice. *Metabolism 46:* 763-68.

Koltyn, K.F. & Morgan, W.P. 1990. Psychological and physiological alterations following whole body cooling and vigorous exercise. *Medicine and Science in Sports and Exercise 22:* 78.

Koltyn, K.F. & Morgan, W.P. 1992a. Influence of underwater exercise on anxiety and body temperature. *Scandinavian Journal of Medicine 26:* 132-34.

Marsden, C.A., Conti, J., Strope, E., Curzon, G., & Adams, R.N. 1979. Monitoring 5-hydroxyytryptamine release in the brain of the freely moving unanethetized rat using in vivo voltammetry. *Brain Research 171:* 85-9.

McMeanamy, R.H. 1965. Binding of indole analogues to human serum albumin. Effects of fatty acids. *Journal of Biological Chemistry 24:* 4235-43.

Mougin, C., et al. 1988. Plasma levels of beta-endorphin, prolactin, and gonadotropins in male athletes after an international Nordic ski race. *European Journal of Applied Physiology 57:* 425-29.

Nathan, R.S., Sachar, E.J., Asns, G.M., et al. 1993. Relative insulin insensitivity and cortical secretion in depressed patients. *Psychiatric Research 4:* 291-300.

North, T.C., McCullagh, P., & Tran, Z.V. 1990. Effects of exercise on depression. *Exercise and Sports Science Reviews 18:* 379-415.

Olehansky, M.A. et al. 1990. The influence of fitness on neuroendocrine responsive to exhaustive treadmill exercise. *European Journal of Pharmacology 59:* 405-10.

Roy, A., Jong, J.D., & Linnoila, M.1989. Cerebrospinal fluid monoamine metabolites and suicidal behavior in depressed patients: A 5-year follow up study. *Archives of General Psychiatry 46:* 609-12

Schildkraut, J.J., & Kety, S.S. 1967. Biogenic amines and emotion. *Science 156:* 21-30.

Scully, D., Kremer, J., et al. 1998. Physical exercise and psychological well being: A critical review. *British Journal of Sports Medicine 32:* 111-20.

Diever, L., & Davis, K.L. 1985. Overview: Toward a dysregulation hypothesis of depression. *American Journal of Psychiatry 142:* 1017-1031.

Simes, W.E. 1988. Discussion: Exercise, Fitness and Mental Health. In R. K. Dishman (Ed.), Exercise, Fitness and Health (pp 627-631). Champaign, IL: Human Kinetics Publishers.

Stein, E.A., & Vomachka, A.J. 1984. Effects of exercise training on brain opium peptides and serum LH in female rats. *Peptides 5*: 953-58.

Tkachuk, G.A. & Martin, G.L. 1999. Exercise therapy for patients with psychiatric disorders: Research and clinical implications. *Professional Psychology: Research and Practice 30, 275-82.*

Walter, M., Knowles, & G., Pogson, I. 1989. How does displacement of albumin-bound tryptophan cause sustained increases in free trypto-phan concentration in plasma and 5-hydroxytryptamine synthesis in the brain? *Biochemistry Journal 262:* 365-368.

Wildmann, J., et al. 1986. Increase in circulating beta-endorphin-like immunoreactivity with the chance in feeling of pleasantness after running. *Life Science, 38*: 997-1003.

Winokur, A. Maislin, G., Phillips, J.K., & Amsterdam, J.D. 1988. Insulin resistance after oral glucose testing in patients with major depres-sion. *American Journal of Psychiatry 145*: 325-30.

Wilson W.M., & Marsden C.A. 1996. In vivo measurement of extra-cellular serotonin in the ventral hippocampus during treadmill run. *Behavioral Pharmacology 7:* 101-4.

Wright, J.H., Jacisn, J.J., Radin, N.A., Bell, R.A. 1978. Glucose metab-olism in unipolar depression. *British Journal of Psychiatry 132*: 386-93.

Chapters 2 and 3

American College of Sports Medicine. 1995. *Guidelines for exercise testing and prescription (5th edition)*. Baltimore, MD: Williams and Wilkins.

American Council on Exercise. 1997. *Personal Training Manual*. San Diego, CA: American Council of Exercise.

Alpert, B., Field, T., Goldstein, S., & Perry, S. 1990. Aerobics enhances cardiovascular fitness and agility in preschoolers. *Health Psychology 9:* 48-56.

Baechle, T.R. & Earle, R.W. (Eds.). 2000. *Essentials of Strength Training and Conditioning (2nd edition)*. Champaign, IL: Human Kinetics Publishers.

Blair, S.N., Jacobs, D.R., & Powell, K.E. 1985. Relationship between exercise or physical activity and other health behaviors. *Public Health Reports 100:* 172-80.

Blair, S.N., Kohl, H.W., & Gordon, N.F., & Paffenbarger, R.S. 1992. Physical activity and health: A lifestyle approach. *Medicine, Exercise, Nutrition and Health 1:* 54-57.

Bourchard, C., Shephard, R.J., & Stephens, T. (Eds.). 1994. *Physical activity, fitness and health*. Champaign, IL: human Kinetics Publishers.

Leon, A.S., & Fox, S.M. 1981. Physical Fitness. In E.L. Wydner (Eds.) *The book of health (pp. 283-341)*. New York: Franklin Watts.

Dishman, R.K. 1982. Compliance/adherence in health-related exercise. *Health Psychology 1:* 237-67.

Dishman, R.K. 1992. Physiological and psychological effects of over-training. In K.D. Brownell, J. Rodin & J.H. Witmore (Eds.), *Eating, body weight, and performance in athletes. disorders in modern society.* (pp. 248-272). Philadelphia: Lea & Febiger.

Pollock, M.L., et al. 1998. The recommended quantity and quality of exercise for developing and maintaining cardiovascular and muscular fitness, and flexibility in health adults. Medicine Science in Sports and Exercise 30: 975-91.

Scheele, K., Harzog, G., Ruthaler, Writh, A., & Wencher, H. 1982. Metabolic adaptation to prolonged exercise. *European Journal of Applied Physiology 41:* 101-6.

Sharky, B.J. 1997. *Fitness and Health: 4th Edition.* Champaign, IL: Human Kinetics Publishers.

Taylor, S.E. 1999. *Health Psychology.* Boston, MA: McGraw-Hill Companies Inc.

Chapter 4

Abou-Saleh, M.T. & Coppen, A. 1986The biology of folate in depression: Implications for nutritional hypotheses of the psychosis. *Journal of Psychiatric Research, 20,* 91-101.

Alpert, J & Fava, M. 1997. Nutrition and depression: The role of folate. *Nutritional Review 13:* 503-14.

Barkman, M., et al. 1989. Effects of fish oil supplementation on glucose metabolism and lipid metabolism in NIDDM. *Diabetes 38:* 1314-19.

Bergstrom, S. & Sjovall, J. 1957. The isolation of prostaglandin. *Acta Chem Scand, 1:* 1086.

Bloomstrand, E. Hassmen, B, & Newholme, E. A. 1991. Effect of amino acid supplementation on mental performance. *Acta Physiologica Scandinavica 143:* 225-6.

Borkman, M., et al. 1993. The relationship between insulin sensitivity and the fatty acid composition of skeletal-muscle phosopholipids. *New England Journal of Medicine 328:* 238-44.

Bourre, J.M., et al. 1993. Function of dietary polyunsaturated fatty acids in the nervous system. *Prostaglandins Leukot Essential Fatty Acids 48:* 5-15.

Brenner, R.R. 1982. Nutrition and hormonal factors influencing desaturation of essential fatty acids. *Progressive Lipid Research 20:* 41-8.

Crellin, R. 1993. Folates and psychiatric disorders: Clinical potential. *Drugs 45:* 623-36.

Edwards, R., Peet, M., Shay, J., & Horrobin, D. 1998. Omega-3 polyunsaturated fatty acid levels in the diet and in red blood cell membranes of depressed patients. *Journal of Affective Disorders 48:* 149-55.

Fava, M., Borus, J., Alpert, J, et al. 1997. Folate, vitamin $B1_{12}$, and homocysteine in major depressive disorder. *American Journal of Psychiatry 154:* 426-28.

Garg, M.L., et al. 1989. Fish Oil prevents change in arachidonic acid and cholesterol content in rat caused by dietary cholesterol. *Lipids 24(4):* 266-270.

Ghadirian, A.M. et al. Folic acid deficiency and depression. 1980. *Psychosomatics 21:* 926-29.

Gubter, E. 1982. Optimal intake of vitamin C for the human organism. *Nutritional Health 1:* 66-77.

Hartman, A., et al. 1995. Vitamin E prevents exercise induced DNA damage. *Mutations Research 346(4):*195-202.

Hibbeln, J.R. 1998. Fish consumption and major depression. *The Lancet 351:* 1213.

Kanof, P.D., et al. 1986Prostaglandin receptor sensitivity in psychiatric disorders. *Archives of General Psychiatry 43:* 987-93.

Maes, M., et al. 1996. Fatty Acid composition in major depression: decreased omega-3 fractions in cholesterol esters and increased C20:4 omega 6/C20:5 omega 3 ratio in cholesterol esters and phosopholipids. *Journal of Affective Disorders 38:* 35-46.

Maes, M. & Smith, R.S. 1998. Fatty acids, cytokins, and major depression. *Biological Psychiatry 43:* 313-14.

Maes, M., et al. 1999. Lowered omega-3 polyunsaturated fatty acids in serum phosopholipids and cholesterol esters of depressed patients. *Psychiatric Research 85:* 275-91.

Malasanos, T.H. & Stacpoole, P.W. 1998. Biological effects of omega-3 fatty acids in diabetes mellitus. *Diabetes Care 14:* 1160-79.

Melanson, K., Greenberg, A., et al. 1998. Blood glucose and hormonal response to small and large meals in health young and older women. *J Geront A, 53:* 8299-8305.

Meador, K.J. 1993. Preliminary findings of high does thiamine in dementia of Alzheimer's type. *Journal of Geriatric Psychiatry Neurology 6:* 222-29.

Metz, S., Fujimoto, W., & Robertson, R.O. 1982. Modulation of insulin secretion by cyclic AMP and prostaglandin E. *Metabolism 31:* 1014-33.

Paolisso, G., et al. 1993. Pharmacological doses of vitamin E improve insulin action in healthy subjects and non insulin-dependent diabetic patients. *American Journal of Clinical Nutrition 57:* 848-52.

Patkinson, A.J. et al. 1994. Elevated concentrations of plasma omega-3 polyunsaturated fatty acids among Alaskan Eskimos. *American Journal of Clinical Nutrition 59:* 389-88.

Peet, M., Murphy, B., Shay, J., & Horrobin, D. 1998. Depletion of omega-3 fatty acid levels in red blood cell membranes of depressive patients. *Biological Psychiatry 43:* 315-9.

Pelikanova, T., et al. 1989. Insulin secretion and insulin action are related to the serum phosopholipids fatty acid pattern in healthy men. *Metabolic Clinical Expermientation.38:* 188-92.

Robertson, W.B., et. al. 1961. Augmentation of collagen synthesis by absorbic acid in vitro. *Biochemistry and Biophysics 49:* 404-6.

Robertson, R.P. 1983. Prostaglandins, glucose homeostasis, and diabetes mellitus. *Annual Review of Medicine 43:* 1-12.

Sadur, C.N., & Echel, R.H. 1982. Insulin stimulation of adipose tissue lipoprotein lipase. *Journal of Clinical Investigation 69:* 1119-23.

Sears, B. 1995. *The Zone.* HarperCollins: New York.

Simopoulos, A.P., Leaf, A., & Salem, N. 1999. Workshop on the essentiality of and recommended dietary intakes for omega-6 and omega-3 fatty acids. *Journal of American College of Nutrition 18:* 487-89.

Stool, A.L. et al. 1999. Omega-3 fatty acid in bipolar disorder: a preliminary double blind, placebo-controlled trial. *Archives of General Psychiatry 56:* 407-12.

Storlien, L.H. 1987. Fish oil prevents insulin resistance induced by high-fat feeding rats. *Science 237:* 885-88.

Tarnopolsky, M.A. MacDougal, J.D. & Atkinson, S.A. 1988. Influence of protein intake and training status on nitrogen balance and lean body mass. *Journal of Applied Physiology 64:* 187-93.

Unger, R.H. 1971. Glucogon and the insulin: glucogon ratio in diabetes and other catabolic illnesses. *Diabetes 20.* 834-38.

Westphal, S.A., Gannon, M.C., & Nutrall, F.Q. 1990. Metabolic response to glucose ingested with various amounts of protein. *American Journal of Clinical Nutrition 62:* 267-72.

Zawadzki, K.M., Yaspelkis, B.B., & Ivy, J.L. 1992. Carbohydrate-protein complex increases the rate of muscle glycogen storage after exercise. *Journal of Applied Physiology 72:* 1854-59.

Chapter 5

Bock, B.C., et al. 1997. Predictors of exercise adherence following participation in a cardiac rehabilitation program. *International Journal of Behavioral Medicine 4:* 50-75.

Bouchard, C., Shephard, R.J., & Stephens, T. (Eds.). 1993. *Physical activity, fitness and health consensuses statement.* Champaign, IL: Human Kinetics Publishers.

Bungum, T.J., Orsak, K.C., & Chung, C.L. 1997. Factors affecting exercise adherence at a worksite wellness program. *American Journal of Health Behavior 21:* 60-6.

Caserta, M.S.& Gillett, P.A. 1998. Older women's feelings about exercise and their adherence to an aerobic regimen over time. *The Gerontologist 38:* 602-609.

Courney, K.S. et al. 1983. Social support and physical health. *Health Psychology 2:* 367-91.

Casperson, C.J., Merritt, R.K., & Stephens, T. 1994. International physical activity patterns: A methodological perspective. In R.K. Dishman (Ed), *Advances in Exercise Adherence* (pp. 73-100). Champaign, IL: Human Kinetics Publishers.

Courneya, K.S. 1995. Understanding readiness for regular physical activity in older individuals: An application of the theory of planned behavior. *Health Psychology 14:* 80-87.

Department of Health and Human Service 1990. *Health people 2000: National health promotion and disease prevention objectives.* (DDHSPHS) 91-50212, p94). Washington, D.C.: U.S. Government Printing Office.

Dishman, R.K. & Ickes, W. 1981. Self-motivation and adherence to habitual physical activity. *Journal of Applied Social Psychology 10*: 115-32.

Dishman, R.K. 1981. Biological influence of exercise adherence. *Research Quarterly for Exercise and Sport 52:* 143-59.

Dishman, R.K. 1982. Compliance/adherence in health-related exercise. *Health Psychology 1:* 237-67.

Dishman, R.K. 1984. Motivation and exercise adherence. In J.M. Silva III & R.S. Weinberg (Eds.). *Psychological Foundations of Sport.* Champaign, IL: Human Kinetic Publishers.

Dishman, R.K. 1987. Exercise adherence and habitual physical activity. In W.P. Morgan & S.E. Goldston (Eds.). *Exercise and Mental Health.* (pp. 57-82). Washington D.C.: Hampshire.

Dishman, R.K. 1988a. *Exercise adherence: Its impact on public health.* Champaign, IL: Human Kinetics Publishers.

Dishman R.K.1988b. Determinants of participation in physical activity. In Bouchard, C., Shephard, R.J., & Stephens, T. (Eds.), *Exercise, fitness and health* (pp.75-102). Champaign, IL: Human Kinetics Publishers.

Dishman, R.K. 1991. Increasing and maintaining physical activity. *Behavior Therapy 22:* 345-378.

Dishman, R.K. 1994b. *Advances in exercise adherence.* Champaign, IL: Human Kinetics Publishers.

Duncan, T.F., & McAuley E. 1993. Social Support and efficacy cognitions in exercise adherence: A latent growth curve analysis. *Journal of Behavioral Medicine 16:* 199-218.

Epstein, L.H., Koeske, R., & Wing, R.R. 1984. Adherence to exercise in obese children. *Journal of Cardiac Rehabilitation 4:* 185-95.

Hammond, J,.M., Brodie, D.A., Bundred, P.E., and Cummins, A. 1995. *Exercise on prescription: an evaluation. A guide for similar schemes based upon the work on the Life Project and the University of Liverpool.* University of Liverpool.

Ingledew, D.K., Markland, D., & Medley, A.R. 1998. Exercise motives and stages of change. *Journal of Health Psychology 3:* 477-89.

Kemmer, F.W. & Berger, M. 1986. Therapy and better quality of life: The dichotomous role of exercise in diabetes mellitus. *Diabetes Metabolism, Rev 2:* 53-68.

Kendzierski, D. 1990. Exercise self-schemata: Cognitive and behavioral correlates. *Health Psychology 9:* 69-82.

King, A.C. 1991. Community intervention for promotion of physical activity and fitness. *Exercise and Sports Science Reviews 19:* 211-60.

Leon, A.S. 1983. Exercise and coronary heart disease. *Hospital Medicine 19:* 38-50.

Lee, C. 1993a. Factors related to the adoption of exercise among older women. *Journal of Behavioral Medicine 16:* 323-34.

Lee, C. 1993b. Attitudes, knowledge, and stages of change. A survey of exercise patterns in older Australian women. *Health Psychology 12:* 476-80.

Lord, J 1994. *Exercise on prescription: does it work.* Stockport: Stockport Health Commission.

Marcus, B.H., & Owen, N. 1982. Motivational readiness, self-efficacy, and decision-making of exercise. *Journal of Applied Social Psychology 22:* 3-16.

Martin, J.E. & Dubbert, P. M. 1982. Exercise applications and promotion in behavioral medicine: Current status and future directions. *Journal of Consulting and Clinical Psychology 50:* 1004-17.

McAuley, E. 1992. The role of efficacy cognitions I the prediction of exercise behavior in middle aged adults. *Journal of Behavioral Medicine 15:* 65-88.

McAuley, E. 1993. Self-efficacy and the maintenance of exercise participation in older adults. *Journal of Behavioral Medicine 16:* 103-13.

McAuley, E. & Courneya, K.S. 1992. Self-efficacy relationships with affective and exertion responses to exercise. *Journal of Social Applied Social Psychology 22:* 312-26.

McAuley, E., Mihalko, S.L., & bane, S.M. 1997. Exercise and self-esteem in middle-aged adults: multidimensional relationships and physical fitness and self-efficacy influences. *Journal of Behavioral Medicine 20:* 67-80.

McEntee, D.J., & Halgin, R.P. 1999. Cognitive Group therapy and aerobic exercise in the treatment of anxiety. *Journal of College Student Psychotherapy 13: 37-55.*

Meyers, R.S. & Roth, D.L. Perceived benefits of and barriers to exercise and stage of exercise adaptation in young adults. *Health Psychology 16:* 277-83.

North, T.C., McCullagh, P., & Tran, Z.V. 1990. Effect of exercise on depression. *Exercise and Sports Science Reviews 18:* 379-415.

Oldridge, N.G. 1982. Compliance and exercise in primary and second-ary prevention of coronary heart disease: A review. *Preventative Medicine 11:* 56-70.

Ryan, R. M., Fredrick, C.M., Lepes, D., Rubio, N., Sheldon, K.M. 1997. Intrinsic Motivation and Exercise Adherence. *International Journal of Sports Psychology* 28: 335-54.

Sallis, J.F., Patterson, T.L., Buono, M.J., Atkins, C.J., & Nadar, P.R. 1988. Aggregation of physical activity habits in Mexican-American and Anglo families. *Journal of Behavioral Medicine 11: 21-42.*

Sallis, J.F. & Hovell, M.F. 1990. Determinants of exercise Behavior. *Exercise and Sports Science Reviews 18:* 307-30.

Sallis, J.F. et. al. 1990. Lifetime history of relapse from exercise. *Addictive Behaviors 15:* 573-79.

Schulz, R. & Decker, S. 1985. Long-term adjustment to physical disability: the role of social support, perceived control, and self-blame. *Journal of Personality and Social Psychology 48:* 1162-72.

Serfass, R.C. & Gerberich, S.G. 1984. Exercise for optimal health. Strategies and motivational considerations. *Preventative Medicine 13:* 79-99.

Sunkin, L.R. & Gross, A.M. 1994. Assessment of coping with high risk situations for exercise relapse among health women. *Health Psychology 13* 274-77.

Taylor, S.E. 1999. *Health Psychology.* Boston, MA: McGraw-Hill Companies Inc.

Wallston B.S., Alagna, S.W., Devellis, B. McE., & Devellis, R.F. 1983. Social support and physical health. *Health Psychology* 2: 367-91.

Wilcox, S. & Storandt, M. 1996. Relations among age, exercise, and psychological variables in a community sample of women. *Health Psychology* 15 110-13.

About the Author

Marcos R. Salazar earned his psychology degree from Amherst College, is a certified personal trainer (CPT) certified by the American Council on Exercise (ACE), a Johnny G. Spin Instructor (JGSI), and is a member of the National Strength and Conditioning Association and American Psychological Association. Salazar has conducted extensive research on exercise, nutrition, and mental health and has presented his results at institutions such as the University of Rochester and Mt. Holyoke College. Salazar has also conducted research on other alternative approaches to depression and has proposed a new, natural supplement treatment in the biomedical journal *Medical Hypotheses* (December 2000).

0-595-20782-0